Born
out
of
Conflict

Cedar Park a/H

Born out of Conflict

THE AUTOBIOGRAPHY OF
BEN SONG
AS TOLD TO CLIFF CHRISTIANS

FOREWORD BY
DALE EVANS ROGERS

ZONDERVAN PUBLISHING HOUSE
GRAND RAPIDS, MICHIGAN

CONTENTS

FOREWORD *by Dale Evans Rogers*

INTRODUCTION *by Cliff Christians*

FOREWORD

I have always appreciated and enjoyed a song, for to me it means harmony, lifting the soul. Not long ago I had the richly rewarding experience of hearing a real song—one of great courage, faith, and inspiration—a *Song* that challenged my life and my faith as a Christian.

This *Song* is a delightful blend of traditional, far-eastern courtesy, with vital, dynamic faith in the goodness and power of the almighty living God and His Christ.

Ben Song came to the Apple Valley Inn, near our home in Apple Valley, California, for dinner one night about a year ago —brought by mutual Christian friends from Canoga Park, California. At that time I learned that he was the first Korean Christian missionary with a permanent visa to the United States. Now, I have a natural empathy for the Korean people, since we had the privilege of adopting a Korean war orphan nine years before the Lord took her home in a church bus accident in 1964. Our own In Ai Lee (Deborah Lee Rogers) was such a blessing to our home that in some way I have always wanted to befriend another of her people.

Being Devotional Chairman of the Church of the Valley, Presbyterian women, I invited *Ben Song* to address our monthly women's meeting. For an hour we heard with incredulous delight, an amazing story of real, early church Christian faith and practice from a grateful Korean—one who not only is grateful to God for His salvation through Jesus Christ, but one who also is deeply grateful to our country for her help to his people. It does something wonderful to the heart to hear a foreigner say "Thank You" to Uncle Sam for needed help—particularly in these days of ingratitude and godlessness on all sides of the globe.

Ben Song's ministry is timely and vital to our country, and indeed, to the world at large. New doors are constantly being opened for him to address high schools, colleges, women's groups, men's groups—doors that are often closed to Christian speakers.

Because *Ben Song* understands political unrest and revolution, he is welcomed as a speaker in many heretofore closed areas, particularly in the educational realm.

"God works in mysterious ways His wonders to perform!" A bright new beam of Eastern gospel light is spreading rapidly over our land, due to this chosen vessel of God. *Ben Song* has a real message of challenging Christian faith that is desperately needed today. May God bless and speed his remarkable ministry.

DALE EVANS ROGERS

Apple Valley, California

INTRODUCTION

Writing this autobiography for Ben has been a spiritual treat for me. And I trust reading it will be for you! Many days of prayer and conversation were shared in forming the book—days in Los Angeles, California; Aspen, Colorado; and Grand Rapids, Michigan.

Ben's story is a miracle of what God can do. Have you any doubt that He's alive today? Every chapter is a testimony of supernatural love. And *power!*

Where is the real fascination in these pages? Perhaps it is the incredible plunge from riches to caves and begging. Perhaps it is the ruggedness of another country at war. Or Ben's wonderful love for the forgotten. Or his dynamic ability to reach teenagers in America. Or his fresh excitement in seeing lives changed by the impact of Jesus Christ. Whatever speaks most to you, we'll thank God for it.

This book is not simply a diary, a list of events. Woven into Ben Song's incredible story are rich insights, words of prophecy and wisdom that will thrill your heart.

CLIFF CHRISTIANS

Grand Rapids, Michigan

Born Out Of Conflict

1

FROM MANSION TO CAVE

§ **"STRONG TORNADOES"** (August 1945)

August 15, 1945! Mighty day in history and memorable to me as well. The Japanese had surrendered; a devastating World War was over. Liberation and new hope made the Koreans ecstatic with joy.

But August 15 was the day of the "tornado" for me. It was a turning point in my destiny—the beginning of the breakup of our family life.

Not too many days later we clenched our teeth and watched helplessly as rifle butts crashed down about my father's head, neck and shoulders. Some local men were taking out their passionate revenge upon my father. He was accused of pro-Japanese activities during the occupation of our country. The men wanted to teach our family a permanent lesson by trying to kill him before our eyes. They tore down the gates, looted our possessions, ravaged our home. How I have longed to put those scenes from my mind!

After more tortures and beatings our attackers ran, leaving my father for dead. Not long before these same men had done his every bidding.

Father was an honored, classed, and wealthy man. For twelve years (1933–1945) he served as the mayor-statesman of Choong Chung province. My great grandfather had been a prime minister during the Ye dynasty.

We lived in a fabulous mansion with seven servants. Everything we could possibly want we had — and more. Our family

13

enjoyed luxuries which only those of the aristocracy were able to have. We even played soccer on our own private football field.

That night after my father's beating was one of those disturbing times filled with dreams and restlessness. The next morning I awoke to learn that during the night my father had fled for fear of his life. The "tornado" of hatred had struck. My father was gone. We never heard from him again.

But the angry men kept coming back to the house. Continually they broke through the gate, smashed into the house and began beating my mother. "Where is your husband?" they demanded as they yanked her head back by her hair.

Though I was only seven, I despised these men more than anything in the world. The way they terrorized my mother was unspeakable, and I wished for a gun so that I could shoot them. Even while she fed and carried a month-old baby, they would persecute her.

They returned again and again. Yet these men never broke my mother's will. She loved her children so much that she was miraculously able to withstand all their vicious treatment.

But the "tornado" of tragedy had no compassion. It was not long before our mother wearied and fell ill. And somehow there seemed to be no doctors around now. We could not find help for her anywhere. I had heard from a Chinese doctor once, that a certain snake would help cure sickness. Boiled together with tree roots, this was supposed to make the finest medicine possible.

My mother was intimately precious to me, so I went into the mountains in search of the snake. For days I braved the cold and danger, but couldn't find a snake anywhere. I was ashamed to return home. Finally mustering up my courage, I left the mountains and went back. My absence had worried her! She hugged and kissed me as if I had actually found a snake and brought it along.

But that night was the last entry in her diary. When I heard the sobbing of relatives from behind her bedroom door, I knew mother had died. They said it was an unknown illness. Certainly death came from a broken heart and crushed spirit. The vicious "tornado" had struck again.

Four of us, three boys and a baby sister now four months old, were orphans! Our beloved parents were gone. Now our home, property, possessions were taken over by the government. There was some law about pro-Japanese activities which permitted this.

Death had come cruelly and viciously to our mother. Nothing could stop the call of the grave. My father's prestige and success meant nothing when death beckoned. The power of mother's love was overwhelming, you would say. Yes, it was, except in the face of death. All the castle walls and iron gates could not restrain it.

We were sent to live with an aunt and uncle. My family had been especially helpful to them during the years, and to their home we went.

§ **"MOM, I NEED YOU"** (December 1945)

Life was heavy. There wasn't much joy anywhere. Our relatives did their best, but the pressures of eight children made everything pretty wearisome and confusing. The arguments and burdens began to mount.

In the primary school I attended, most kids had parents and happy homes. They played games, told jokes, had fun. But not I. It seemed I had no laughter left in me.

One of the rooms in the house was set aside as a worship area for ancestors. Following Confucius meant having a healthy respect for families. Confucianism is not a religion, but a philosophy with many high ideals. The major emphasis was on respect for authority. We were taught to obey the king, our parents, our elders. This meant, as well, a full reverence for those in our family who had died. Every day we put out fresh rice in the worship room for our ancestors' spirits if they wished to eat. Much of our time was spent in this kind of worship.

But I hated the ancestor worship room. It was so creepy in there, so dark and spooky. So instead of worshiping my ancestors, I went to the grave of my mother. Before long this became a habit. In a year's time, I visited this grave more than 300 times. I looked at my cousins and saw how their mother cared for them. Then I would run out to the grave again and cry out for my mom to come back to life. I needed her. My brothers did, too, but especially my baby sister.

One night in particular my heart was especially heavy. I walked the two miles to the mountain grave, so discouraged that I felt my heart would break. I fell down by the grave on my knees. "Mom, where are you? I need you. I keep coming because I want you." I called again and again, until after midnight. But no answer came. The only sound was the wind blowing against my cheek.

The weather turned cold and it started to snow. Before long the entire graveyard and my shoulders were covered with snow. My cheeks began to freeze. But they didn't hurt as much as the ache in my heart.

My little brother was asleep when I came home again. He was lying there in innocence. And it made me think. Why do certain countries have the ravages of war? Why were these bloody battles part of our destiny? If war had never started, I would still have a home and a mother. Why did God allow this to happen to us?

As I recall it now, my mother taught me so much about life. She was the symbol of patience. Her children meant days and years of time: feeding, washing diapers, training, teaching many basics about life. Who waited for us when we returned home from school, and dressed us with an extra sweater when it was cold, and brought us medicine when we were sick and an extra blanket when we were uncomfortable at night? She did!

But our mother never asked her children for a reward. Under heaven, whose love was like my mom's love? Whose love had more depth and richness? Whose love could show more sacrifice? I think of her motherly, dedicated love as an example of the way God wants all of us to live today.

§ **"POOR BABY SISTER"** (November 1946)

Every day was trying and extremely difficult. There was a scarcity of food. Our coming into the home of our relatives proved a real burden to everyone. Life didn't hold much hope and promise.

There was no milk for my baby sister, so we tried to make some from rice. My aunt became so desperate she constantly yelled at me: "Make that kid stop crying." By boiling water with rice in it, we could prepare something nourishing. But it must be boiled exactly the proper length of time. If the time is too short, the liquid becomes undrinkable. If it was boiled too long, it burned and had a terrible smell.

I was the one who had to care for the baby. Since I was only eight years old, it was difficult to prepare the rice water just right. My sister would take a little of it, and then throw it up. Her body could not accept this food. Yet we could not waste precious rice by throwing away the juice if it was over- or under-cooked. My baby sister was becoming weaker. She cried incessantly. Nothing I did seemed to help. I held her constantly and tried to comfort her. I put her on my back, cradled her in my arms, sat by her bed, but nothing made her content. Imagine a baby crying for hours at a time. No wonder my aunt lost control and yelled out that we must do something.

The house in which we lived was one big room shaped like a T. There was little privacy. One day as I watched my sister, I heard my aunt threaten us and say: "I can't live with you anymore." The meaning of this phrase in Korean is really terrible. It slammed against my heart like a hammer. This was the final curse that one relative could give to another. I couldn't keep back my tears.

Well, it was not long before my little sister died. All of our crude efforts to save her had failed. Perhaps you have never seen a child die of starvation, but it is one of the ugliest sights imaginable. No one wanted even to touch her body.

Finally my elder brother and I mustered our courage, found a paper box, put her body in it and took her out to the mountain.

At the time, I was only nine years old, but the scar of this experience remains today. Every shovel of dirt was covered with tears. The ground was frozen so hard we could not get the grave any deeper than three feet. Finally we put all her clothes and her few toys in the box with the body and buried her. But somehow we could not leave the place. We stayed there nearly all night, until at last we left for home exhausted. Our little sister was gone.

§ **"MY FIRST BEGGING"** (February 1947)

That evening at the mountain, as we cried and lived the pain of giving a loved one to the grave, we decided that we would have to leave our relative's home. I was the one who first suggested it. Every desire to stay and look for new hope with them had vanished. Their indifference and lack of sympathy was too much to bear.

Not many days later we were ready. It was just the three of us now—my older and younger brothers and myself. For hours we trudged north to another county, thirty miles in all. My little brother did not want to come, so we just dragged him along with us. There were all sorts of rocks and sharp stones along the path. Many times we stumbled and often we stopped to rest. Finally we found a cave in the mountainside and were exhausted enough to see it as our future home. It was near an army base.

You will probably never know how good a meal from a garbage can tastes. I do. There seemed to be plenty of them near the camps of the United Nations forces. But then several weeks later, the military must have changed its policy. No longer could we find the garbage set out any more. This placed us under a terrible hardship.

I saw some other people begging and I began to realize that it was the only possibility left. I even revolted at the thought of begging. To beg is to be less than human. But I had to do it. My younger brother would plead with me: "Can't you get me some food? I'm so hungry." His words cut me like a sword. I was hungry, too, but I could restrain myself. As he kept insisting, I had no alternative but to go out and beg.

The first lady I met tried to pass me by. But I asked her for a nickel anyhow. She refused! "You don't look like a beggar boy to me." I persisted: "Please give me a nickel." Finally she opened her purse and threw a nickel to the ground in disgust. "Next time you had better work," she said. I didn't want to stoop so low as to pick the coin from the dust, but finally I reached down and took it for myself. The tears were streaming down my cheeks. I cursed her and I cursed society.

"Why do you cry?" she screamed. "Didn't I give you a nickel? Do you need another one?" I didn't answer. Undoubtedly she never understood how deeply the experience and her words had seared my soul.

In the days ahead I spent some time as a shoeshine boy. This was not easy either. But living on the brink of starvation sometimes makes a person do almost anything. I was proud of my heritage and resented the cruelty of life. Yet somehow we managed to struggle on. Live? We did not live. We could not die, so we existed.

Everything seemed like one big shadow. But even in all the darkness and sorrow, I realized deep down that there is always some sunshine. I knew I must fight back. I knew I had to grit my teeth and determine to move ahead. Even as an underprivileged beggar boy, I must not despair. Even if everyone cursed me, I knew I would not fail. Even a rat hole has an opening.

2

A FLOW OF BLOOD

§ "A FLOW OF BLOOD" (June 1950)

Sunday, June 25, 1950, had scarcely dawned when the silence was shattered with the booming of guns. The peaceful air and earth seemed to vibrate with the thunder of cannons. The wretchedly familiar sounds of war prevailed in our country again.

The capital city of Seoul, thirty miles from the cave we called home, was besieged by the North Korean Communists. The attack occurred with such suddenness that even our town officials were not informed. The invading army had advanced almost unseen. What a shock when, a few days later, the Communist soldiers completely took over our town.

Fire seemed to be shooting out from everywhere. The airplanes were particularly frightening. One plane, for example, dropped a bomb not ten feet from where we were standing. At that point a miracle happened and the bomb didn't go off. Everywhere else bombs were exploding and killing people, but the one near us did not go off. By the grace of God, we were not hurt. I live today to testify to His protecting care.

No one wanted war. We in South Korea despised the very thought of it. No one wanted to kill and be killed. We rebelled at the wars fought in history. Yet there was war, almost constantly. From the Garden of Eden until now there had been fighting between individuals and nations. Perhaps, I concluded, there was something wrong with human nature itself.

§ "SO-CALLED PEACE POLITICAL PARTY" (July 1950)

Before the Communists invaded, there were seven different political parties in Korea. Several of them were always radical, always protesting the government. They never showed much love for the people or the country. After the Communists moved in, these people were the ones who became their leaders. It was important to the Communist invasion, because these people knew the citizens intimately and could provide the information that was necessary.

Within a few short weeks the invaders, and those from South Korea who supported them, set up a triangular secret police system. As soon as they came into an area, they ordered everyone to register within three days. Each was then given a registration card. People were watched so closely that it would be unsafe to travel if you did not carry that card. And no one other than the communist military was allowed on the streets after eight p.m. Even during the day time anyone 14 years and over had to carry a registration card.

By this arrangement, every person in sympathy with the Communist cause was assigned to spy on two other people. As a result everyone lived in constant fear. You could not trust a single person. Even families were torn apart. Husbands could not be sure of their wives, and vice versa. It seemed that the minute any information was shared by a person, the secret police knew about it. Even family ties were not considered sacred.

As one example, let me tell you about a little woman who was a worker for the Oriental Missionary Society in the southwestern part of Korea. The Communist guerrillas were very strong there during the Korean War. During those years, she was busy leading a church in the area.

Strangely enough, her brother became a member of the people's peace party and lived like a guerrilla in the rural back country. Under the impetus of the Communist invasion of South Korea this man came down out of the mountains and searched for this Christian lady, his sister. When he found her, he chopped off her hands because they were hands that had so often held a Bible. Then he gouged out her eyes because they were eyes that had so often read the Word of God. Then he mutilated her body and killed her.

Even the rest of my family was torn apart. Long before the invasion, one of my brothers was involved in these political groups. He was typical of the young people captivated by these movements. Our family had already undergone so much struggle he wanted to rise above that and achieve equality.

Out of this, a serious problem developed between my two brothers. The oldest wanted to continue the heritage and long-standing Korean customs. The younger sympathized with the Communists. Right after the invasion he was killed fighting for them on the front lines.

The wolf never shows his real attitude. Hidden away in the other political parties, the Communists were living under a sheep's cover. Unrighteousness had veiled itself in programs, organizations, publicity so as to hide its real purpose.

Righteous causes, of course, have meaning inherent in themselves. They do not have to depend on a cover or a method. Since they have purpose and power in themselves, they need not even speak up. They are valid without a front.

This fact had caused the difficulty. Because unrighteousness operated on publicity, it made itself appear to everyone as the strong and powerful. Even though in the end righteousness alone will prevail, it appeared to people in our country as though unrighteousness was really the leader.

§ "HORRIBLE KILLINGS" (August 1951)

The Communist aggression across the 38th parallel brought some of the worst atrocities in the course of world history. The invaders had no sooner arrived than they began the deadly task of determining who were to be put to death.

Any official, any educated, or classed person was immediately marked for execution. One method they used to determine the hierarchy of individuals was to have them extend their hands out, palms up. Those who had smooth hands, hands that didn't show any signs of labor, were judged by the invaders to be of the aristocracy. These would be summarily executed. Those whose hands were rough, hard and calloused, found favor with the Communists. Surely these were farmers or good production people, they assumed.

Christians did not escape the judgment of the Communists either. They took their places along with the others as they were herded into local buildings. These buildings were then sprinkled with gasoline and set ablaze. The cries of the burning humans will never leave my memory.

Perhaps my other brother was one who was killed in this way. At least, he was well known as an anti-Communist youth leader.

I knew it was not safe for me to remain in town, so I decided to hide out in the mountains. My route to the hills was cluttered everywhere with the bodies of my murdered countrymen. Often there was nothing else I could do but walk over the corpses that lay in my path.

When I arrived in the mountains, my heart sank in disbelief. There was no peace and safety here either. The Communists were everywhere, always with drawn bayonets. I worked my way with extreme caution through the countryside. At long last I found refuge at a little farm. There the kindly owners gave me food and a bed in return for my helping them with the chores.

The persecutions of our people continued. My friend, Johnny Lee, writes about them in his book, *A Korean the Communists Could Not Kill.* He describes graphically one of the many horrible murders inflicted on our people:

> Perhaps the worst murder-method I ever witnessed was death by tongue nailing. I saw three men executed by this method. Here is how it would happen: The Communists laid the men, stomach down, on the floor. Their hands and feet were firmly tied. Then the soldiers used a bamboo-clip pliers to pull the victims' tongues out to the nth degree. (I never knew, until then, how long the human tongue is.) When the tongue was out to its full length, the Communists hammered a nail through it into the floor. The screams of these victims were indescribable.

Rev. Park was the father of one of my friends. He escaped from North Korea where he was doing missionary work. Later he was apprehended in South Korea and given a mock trial by the Communists. They said they would let the people decide the fate of Rev. Park at his trial. He was accused of being an insurrectionist. He was asked, "Are you a Christian?"

He replied, "Yes, with all my heart and soul I am a Christian."

"Tell us, Mr. Park," they jeered, "what does it mean when you say that you are a Christian?"

"It means that I believe in Jesus Christ, that He is my Saviour. But is it a crime to think that way?"

Angry voices from the crowd yelled, "Kill him." Others cried, "Cut out his tongue." This was a typical Communist chant, often used in the form of catcalls to incite the group to take revenge.

They cut his tongue from his mouth, spit on him, beat him,

cut open his body. He died with his arms outstretched, his body forming the shape of a cross. But to the end he testified of Jesus. And his testimony made a profound impact on my Confucianist heart.

Hundreds of Christians were submitted to all forms of hideous persecutions for a crime the Communists consider their greatest threat: possessing a heart dedicated to Jesus. On a typical day, dozens of Christians would be forced into a common grave. Shovels of dirt were then heaped upon them until they were buried alive. As it became apparent that General MacArthur and the United Nations Armies were closing in on the Communists, they could not take the time to kill each individual separately. They speeded up the pace to mass proportions to be sure their enemies would go down to defeat with them.

The blessed day that General MacArthur and the United Nations forces liberated us, many Christians came out of their hiding places, and the church bells all over town rang out the happy news. My thoughts ran back to my mother. How proud she would be if I were to attend church.

Mother's family had been one of the first in Korea to become Christians. The year was 1895. But because my father was a Confucianist, he forbade her attendance at church meetings. She was never permitted to impart its precepts to us boys. She revered her Bible, and many, many times, as she was working about her kitchen, I would hear her singing hymns too.

Christians, like mother and Rev. Park, seemed almost happy to go to their deaths. As I pondered these things, I felt there must be much more to Christianity than I knew about. Yes, the freedom bells were ringing, and mother would want me to go to church.

I walked up the steps cautiously and peeked into the sanctuary filled with people. These people had beautiful clothing! I looked at the rags that hung from my hollowed shoulders, acutely aware of how dirty they were. And my bare feet were filthy. No, I could not go in there. I was a beggar boy and my appearance showed it.

In a surge of self analysis I realized what I had become—one of the least. A few years ago I had been one of the gentry, but no more. I clenched my fist and cursed society and even God that He had allowed this to happen to me.

§ **"THE SEED MUST DIE"** (September 1951)

I must tell you the story of Rev. Yang Won Son. His is another gripping account from Korea's wars and struggles with Communism.

This great man had been working on a leper island for a number of years. But when the Japanese overran Korea he was put into prison. He had refused to accept their great Shinto worship, even though Shinto had been made the national God of the Japanese. Rev. Son was not released from the prison until the liberation of Korea in 1945.

Immediately he went back to the leper island. No one wanted to go there. It was one of the worst places in the whole world. But he was eager to go back. For his loving work he became known as a saint and his fame spread across the country of Korea.

There was no school on the leper island. When it was time for his sons to go to college, Rev. Son sent them away from the island to a big city in southern Korea. The young men were active in the school as Christians and showed a clear commitment to Christ.

As the Communists moved into South Korea, the guerrillas were active throughout the country. Some of them made a surprise invasion of the town where Rev. Son's children were attending college. Their movements were so swift that no one was able to flee. Fellow classmates who favored the Communists killed both of the boys out of hatred for their religion.

A few months later General Hodge was pushing the drive toward the mountains and the north. As the city was liberated, the murderer of Rev. Son's sons was captured. The information was forwarded to the Korean General Kim, who was empowered to act during war as governor of that area. General Kim called Rev. Son and informed him that the killer had been captured and would be put to death.

Rev. Son refused permission. He asked to adopt the boy instead. General Kim was stunned. In fact, he would not believe it and started preparations to kill the murderer. Undoubtedly Rev. Son was insane anyhow, he thought. But Dr. Syngman Rhee heard the story and intervened. Since he was a Christian, he understood and allowed Rev. Son to adopt the boy on probation as he requested. Nine months later the Chinese Communists invaded South Korea in renewed force. Rev. Son was captured by the Communist party because he was active in Christian work. They knew he was responsible for the change of his adopted son who was an active member of the student underground Communist party. Finally they killed him in front of many imprisoned Christians.

But the seed which died bore fruit. The boy continued to live with Mrs. Son. He learned the way of salvation and made his personal commitment to Christ. Today he is the pastor of a large Orthodox Presbyterian Church.

I had never met Rev. Son, but I have talked with his adopted son. His story touched my heart. This is only one example of dozens of lepers, haters, Confucianists who accepted Christ through Rev. Son. He never realized all who were influenced by him, including myself. He didn't always see the results. But his sacrifice of life sprang up into changed lives for hundreds of others.

Mr. Ben Song visiting the grave of Rev. Son's two boys.

3

A NEW FAMILY

§ **"BOY WITHOUT A TOMORROW"** (January 1952)

Our country enjoyed freedom once again after the defeat of the Japanese in World War II. But the freedom was short lived. Before long, the Chinese Communists were invading and history marked the beginning of the horrible Korean War in which so many American men would die.

With the encroachment of the enemy, all who were able fled still further south. I joined the crowds. One day I found myself in Pusan, one of the southernmost cities, wandering in the street. It was an aimless wandering. I didn't have the faintest idea of what to do or where to go next.

Apparently it was quite evident that I was afraid and hungry. At least some young boys approached me and asked: "Are you hungry? Are you scared?" They seemed friendly and concerned enough so I followed their lead. Undoubtedly there would be some food wherever they were going.

I realize all of the implications now, but at the time I was innocently led to the headquarters of the beggar boys. They gave me food and shelter all right. Then it became clear what they wanted of me! Theirs was a highly-organized operation and I was the newest recruit. With care and expertise I was taught how to pick pockets, steal, and commit all the other crimes that were necessary to keep the organization moving. I became a puppet to the leaders' demands.

Knowing I had fallen into such a trap sickened me. Begging for food was one thing. At least it seemed permissible to keep oneself from starving. But to commit criminal acts was repugnant to me. I entertained many thoughts of quitting, but trying to do so was hopeless. Once you were involved in a gang, it was impossible to leave voluntarily.

Each city had gangs. Some had many of them. The gangs all had captains who were overseers of the boys' activities. They received a cut of each boy's takings. The captains each had a judge over them who scrutinized all their activities and received a share of the loot as well. Any boy, any age, who was capable of "performing the art" was permitted to join. The gang members' requirements were high, but hundreds of youngsters became involved. They were either "invited" or hijacked into the circle. The girls equivalent to this were prostitutes who operated on the same organizational plan.

For the members who really sacrificed and worked hard it was a wonderful method. Everyone would help each other, trust each other, and live as one family. The ties were closer than you could find in the church. It was the best friendship anywhere, even superseding relatives or society as a whole. They operated on the ethic that the only good acts were those which helped all the members of the beggar boys' gangs. This made for a tightly knit and highly protective group. Whenever one of the gang was hurt, everyone went out together to see that the "wrong" was made right.

One day we were to meet at the train depot to do our usual amount of pickpocketing, stealing and begging. A wave of self-hatred and dismay at the turn my life had taken swept over me. *What am I doing here anyhow?* I asked myself. I jumped on the last car of a departing train and congratulated myself that I would go to another town and be free of the beggar boy gang forever.

I jumped off at the next stop. But that town's gang was waiting for me. A message had been sent ahead. I was questioned thoroughly, but for hours refused to admit my former connections. They beat me and forced me to tell all the facts. Finally, when they had the whole story, they promptly herded me back to the club in Pusan. There was an honor system among these gangs that one group could not steal a "worker" from another.

I had good cause to tremble as I stood before my superiors. Because I had forsaken the gang, my sentence was stiff: I was to be killed that evening at eight o'clock. It would be dark by then. I had committed the unforgivable crime of trying to escape.

I was in agony knowing that eight o'clock was fast approaching. The membership was anxious, too, as the last bit of sunlight dropped behind the horizon. All of a sudden, in surged the police. In their quest to find the murderer of a policeman, they rounded up all of us and took us to headquarters for questioning. I had missed death by ten minutes!

After each of us had been interrogated, we were placed in different orphanages according to our religious backgrounds, or the lack of them. God had plans for me then, even in the lowly state to which I had fallen. He rescued me for in His grace He had determined that He could use me. This is the point at which my life took a miraculous turn, the opposite direction from which it had been plummeting for seven years.

§ "A NEW FAMILY" (October 1953)

The first orphanage in which I was placed proved to be a rather unhappy experience. The chain of disappointments that had plagued my life continued. The director and his family ate and lived well. They operated like business men, seeming to be in the work for profit. Instead of living a life of sacrifice and showing love, they lived in luxury.

For the most part, we kids were given only enough to supply our basic physical needs, and little or no attention. The fact that it was a Buddhist orphanage complicated things too. My Confucian background rebelled against it.

By the amazing providence of God I met a school teacher, Mr. Song, who took a special interest in me. He introduced me after a while to a lovely lady, Mrs. Julia Hahn. Mrs. Hahn had attended Biola College in Los Angeles and was now serving the Lord full time in Korea with her husband Richard.

It was the combined efforts of these two precious souls which enabled me to go to the Isabelle orphanage—a Christian home for the homeless like myself. There were at least twenty other beggar boys in the orphanage, but I didn't really feel at home until much later. The hundreds of babies, symbols of a wartorn land, reminded me too much of my past years and home.

But for the first time in years, I had a full stomach. I was also tremendously pleased with good, fresh clothing. They were far too big, coming from the big people of America for the little people of Korea. But a few cut-offs here and there, a tightening of the belt and they fit fine. It was a proud time for me to be among people where love was shown. The attentiveness and concern of the Hahns made the whole experience a happy event instead of a frightening drudgery.

The Hahns gave me my first precious New Testament. We received religious instruction and learned the doctrines, and we heard about the wonders of God. For the first time I was told about John 3:16, "God so loved Ben Song." I was struck. Did He really love me? The world was cruel. Any show of love was comforting indeed to an orphan like me.

Yes, I learned everything well; my mind showed it had excellent retention. I had a wonderful "knowledge" of Christianity before long. But I didn't realize that it had to reach to my heart, that it had to become part of my very being to become truly meaningful. I was still, in my heart, a "Confucian Christian." My Confucian background had taught me that I had to be good and to do good before I was worthy of approaching God.

§ **"MY NEW JOB"** (September 1954)

I was assigned a unique duty at the orphanage — that of burying dead babies. So many of the little ones were in terrible shape when they came to us. A large number were no more than two days old when they were brought to us, and the greatest percentage of these died. Others were so starved and neglected that they were beyond saving.

So many died that the memory even today is almost too great to bear. The personnel could hardly stand to bury them so they gave me the task. I did it because I felt in some small way, I was paying homage to the sweet baby sister I had lost and had to bury. Since many of the babies had no birthdate or name, I put my name "Song" on them. Over a hundred were buried with that name. I estimate that I laid to rest more than two hundred babies during my stay at the orphanage.

I worked hard for the babies who stayed alive too. There was no running water. Thousands of buckets of water per week had to be taken from the well. All clothing had to be washed by hand. In twelve years time, over 3,000 children grew up in that orphanage. You can't imagine how many diapers that takes!

These babies had a right to eat. They had a right to live. Maybe there were adults who were also hungry and poor, even though they were healthy enough to work. To them our country certainly did not owe the same responsibility. The babies deserved special compassion and love. These were innocent victims of a terrible war and disease.

§ **"DAY OF GRADUATION"** (July 1955)

Living in the orphanage was one thing, but getting an education meanwhile was far more difficult. I wanted very much to attend school and learn the things a normal boy would know. I had two difficulties: How could my education be financed? How could I find the time for it?

I solved my first problem by spending many hours in the mountains cutting wood for sale. I would also give blood just as often as I dared, since it was so needed in our country. These efforts gave me enough financial backing to survive.

Finding the time for school was a more serious problem. Because we lived without personal cost in the orphanage, we were expected to assist by helping with the work. There were thousands of duties for us who were older and healthy. My normal routine was to work in the orphanage all day and study in school at night.

One day during those demanding and turbulent years, a happy event occurred that was to affect my life and direction until today. I was adopted as a foster child by Mr. and Mrs. Herb Woehl of Los Angeles, California. Every month they sent ten dollars for my support. This provided tremendous relief. Without their spiritual and financial encouragement, the course of my life would have been completely different.

By persistent and hard work I was able to graduate from high school at the normal time—only one year behind my age group. That day of commencement was a wonderful one. Parents came from everywhere to share the happiness of their sons and daughters. Everyone was taking pictures, eating lunches together, having fun.

But no one was very excited about me. I stood alone along the sidewalk. In my efforts to achieve my goal, I had been almost a slave, but there were no congratulations. Not a single person in the whole city seemed to care. I took my graduation papers and went off to a park by myself. The tears ran down my cheeks as once again I felt the terrible loneliness and emptiness of living without a family.

I was able to recover my composure, however. That day I resolved not to let the ache in my heart stand in the way. I would go on to school and become a success in life. Perhaps it would be engineering or a profession. At any rate, I vowed to succeed no matter what. Even if no one cared that I had made it this far, I would go further and at least prove satisfactory to myself.

The usual procedure in Korean orphanages is to ask a person to leave "home" upon reaching the age of seventeen. These young people must move on to make opportunity for the endless line of young humanity that is waiting to be admitted.

Seventeen is just an arbitrary age for this exodus to occur. At that age, one is usually not trained to work or handle a trade. His only recourse is to drift back into the old environment of the slum district or find some craftier way of supporting himself.

I was blessed. When it came time for me to leave the orphanage, my adopted parents continued to support me financially. It was their faithful prayers and financial support that helped me finish my education. I attended Seoul Bible College of the Oriental Missionary Society. Three years later my Th.B. degree was granted from the Korean Presbyterian Seminary.

I knew I wanted to become involved in doing God's work, but before I could, God had some work to do in my heart. Only then would He be able to use me.

§ **"NEW BIRTHDAY"** (February 1958)

Most people are not as fortunate as I have been in having two births. My second birth is far more significant to me than my first in that it assures me of everlasting life beyond my physical death.

Like a physical birth, my spiritual birth has a set of statistics:

> Name: Benjamin C. Song
> Birthdate: February 22, 1958
> Birthplace: A mountain in Korea

Let me continue my story of how God so lovingly and carefully prepared my heart to know His Son, Jesus Christ. At this time in my life I thought all I needed was to try to do good things to be in His favor. Thus I was constantly busy in religious activities, organizing projects and workers, conducting youth and church meetings. Though I had been baptized, I felt that something was lacking.

Then at one of our meetings, the speaker, Rev. Kremer, gave his personal testimony. His story was filled with the wondrous things that had happened in his life since he had "accepted Christ" and from then on allowed Him to control his life. He spoke of letting the Holy Spirit guide his hours and days. In all of my religious dedication I had never experienced the wondrous things he told us.

After the meeting, kindly Rev. Kremer listened attentively as I related the doubts about my own spiritual life. He suggested that we find the answers to my soul-search by looking together into the Scriptures. He opened the Bible and we delved into the unchanging Word of God.

He brought I John 1:9 to my attention: "If we confess our sins, he is faithful and just to forgive us our sins, and to cleanse us from all unrighteousness." I had never realized before how great this passage really was. No matter what my wrongs have been, no matter how far down the ladder of degradation I had fallen, if I would sincerely confess my sins and resolve to engage in them no longer, He would forgive and forget my iniquity completely.

The next passage we read together was John 1:12: "But as many as received him, to them gave he power to become the sons of God, even to them that believe on his name." What a thrill to know that we only must believe in Jesus to become a member of His family. What a precious Gospel it appeared to me as God invited me to be His own, laying down no other requisites than faith in His Son. "For by grace are ye saved through faith; and that not of yourselves, it is the gift of God" (Ephesians 2:8).

I had to realize that we cannot earn our way to heaven by doing good, or living by the Ten Commandments, or regularly attending church. God told me plainly that only by accepting His Son, the Lord Jesus Christ, and submitting to His direction would I be assured of eternal life. Salvation is a gift from God. To have it one only has to accept it from Him through one's surrendered will.

And then there was Revelation 3:20: "Behold, I stand at the door, and knock: if any man hear my voice, and open the door, I will come in to him, and will sup with him, and he with me." This was Jesus inviting any man into His fellowship. It became clear that He was not asking whether I was good, or a Caucasian, or a church member. My acceptance with Him did not hinge on that at all. No! He was telling me to come, no matter what I was, or what color, or status, or spiritual condition. There was no barrier to keep me from Him, if my heart was seeking Him.

How objective I had made Christianity by having only "head knowledge" of its contents! The very essence of Christianity is subjective—it has to become a personal relationship with Jesus Christ. Here was a religion described to me as a religion of heart to heart. All the intellectual knowledge one could acquire could not give the eternal life. Satan, for example, knows more about Jesus and salvation than we do. But it only damns him more. How wonderful to learn that I was saved by grace and through faith in Him and His Son. It was not by the amount of Scripture I knew, the volume of reading, the work I had done. I learned about God and the Trinity but I did not know Jesus Christ personally. In other words, I had a head knowledge but I didn't have a right relationship with Him through personal experience. I knew what I believed but now I know in whom I believe and trust. Faith alone, faith alone, faith alone. These words finally penetrated their significance to my soul. The concept of being born again was, at last, a secure and refreshing reality in my life.

It occurred to me that my life had paralleled that of Nicodemus. He was a studious, learned man, a man of the synagogue, trusted, honored, with a great knowledge of the religion he propagated. Yet, he did not comprehend what Jesus meant when He said, "Ye must be born again." I had to learn, as he did, that to be part of a religious persuasion does not in itself make one automatically a child of God. Being born again occurs only when we have permitted Jesus to take His rightful place in our lives. After that we reach a point in making our decisions whereby we are guided by what is God's way and "what must I do" rather than "what do I want?"

I recall the joyousness of the Holy Spirit taking over my soul as I asked Jesus to come into my heart. As Rev. Kremer ministered to me, I knew that nothing is comparable to being under the protective wings of God's love and will.

Typical beggar boy's cave home. Live? We just existed.

Rescued by a missionary lady to live in the Christian Boys Home.

Street meeting. I was 19 years old, a busy religious worker . . . yet lost.

4

THE GREAT COMMISSION

§ **"INTO ARABIA"** (March 1958)

The next day after my conversion, I went into the mountains for prayer and meditation. Thus began some of the greatest wrestling with God I have ever done. I wanted to be faithful to Him and to His Word. I wanted to know His will for my life and then I intended to go out to do it with courage and joy.

On the fifth day, between four and five o'clock in the afternoon, God in His glory extended more of His grace and gave to my heart the following Scripture: "Go ye. Preach the gospel unto all the world. Lo, I am with you always." This is exactly what Jesus had spoken to His disciples after He had risen. These were His final words to them. These instructions were given so they might know how to be obedient to Him. Now God was giving the same commands to me!

This was followed by the words of Matthew 25:40, "Verily I say unto you, Inasmuch as ye have done it unto one of the least of these my brethren, ye have done it unto me." In this Scripture, God told me plainly to whom He wanted me to minister— to the "least of these." I searched my experience. Who were the least of these? It had to be the unfortunate and underprivileged of the slum areas. Praise God, I had emerged from there. Now He wanted me to return.

That very hour I descended from the mountain. God had answered my prayer. In clear and persuasive terms He had given the Great Commission to me personally. I could not waste any more time. He had instructed me to go.

I was now returning to the city's slum area voluntarily. A few years before I could hardly wait to leave it. Now I could hardly wait to enter. No one could have convinced me that of my own volition I would come back to this wretched environment. The most ludicrous part of it all is underscored by my purpose for returning. No one in a million years could have guessed it then. I was coming now to bring the message of Jesus Christ!

The Bible shows how the priest and the Levite do not understand the wounded Jew. Their mansion life was never bothered with that. But the lowly Samaritan catches on immediately. He knows exactly what life is on the everyday, practical level.

The older most often do not understand the younger. And certainly the reverse is true. The Westerner does not really know the Oriental, nor the Oriental the Westerner. And many times this is true even in the church. Members do not understand those outside, or those of a differing social class.

God knew how true this principle was, so He sent me to the underprivileged. I had walked in their shoes and lived their kind of life. I knew what agonies they had to suffer, what their fears were, and what their language said. Only an orphan really understands the loneliness and torment of an orphan.

§ "MACEDONIAN CALL" (October 1958)

The beggar boys were my first target. It wasn't easy, of course, to gain entrance and acceptance. "What are you doing here?" Their words were cold and forbidding. "Why have you come? To spy on us?" They strongly suspected that I was a spy or undercover agent for the police. They reminded me in no uncertain terms that this was the easiest way to get killed.

Calling on my past experience, I was able to communicate with them with relative ease. This made them wonder if the captain of another beggar-boy gang had sent me. Their unique slang and customs were still clear in my memory, so I used every possible tactic to gain their acceptance and dispel their uncertainties. But it took nights of sleeping with them, eating their kind of food, and hours of seemingly meaningless conversation for me to convince the "boys" I had come in friendship.

The first time I had been captured by them. Now the love and message of Jesus Christ were capturing them instead. As God worked out the circumstances through me, His ambassador, I was able to bring the message to hundreds. Before too many weeks we had a small meeting in progress. Just for them to realize that someone cared about them and their destinies produced a genuine rapport.

Now just a few years later, hundreds of neglected and abused souls have been cleansed and renewed by God Himself. A miraculous harvest has been reached. Hundreds now come to the rallies on Thursday night. Thirty of the worst have been baptized and become members of Seoul churches. Nine are attending night school, and one a university. Hundreds have been challenged to find honorable jobs—and they have done so. And everyone stands as an absolute miracle of God, without any pushing from us.

§ **"A PROSTITUTE WITHOUT AN ARM"** (May 1959)

Today I received an impressive letter that I wish to share with you. Someone had been listening to my radio program and wrote in to give her life's story and reaction to the message I preached that day:

"I am a prostitute. At least others have called me that. And I guess it's really true. Perhaps you don't know what a prostitute is. Let me explain. A prostitute is a person who uses her body to make money for herself and others. She is willing to do anything for the sake of a payment in dollars. It's an unusual job to say the least.

"But do you know why I have to be a prostitute? Well, I have always desired friends and the good life. But during the war I lost my brothers and sisters, and my parents. Many of my best friends were killed as well. During some of the same bloodshed, I lost my arm. The bomb that killed others took only an arm, but it could just as well have taken my life. I started to hate myself. I was only fifteen. And a young girl of fifteen does not look too inviting with only one arm.

"The pain and the shock of those first days in the hospital were almost unbearable. There was not a person anywhere who seemed to understand what I was going through. But then when I was released I found that nobody wanted me! That was absolutely more than I could take. I could not find a job anywhere. No matter how much I begged and pleaded, no one was willing to use a handicapped worker.

"I was terribly hungry after some days of this kind of frustration. So I went into the slum area to see if there were any contacts or food available there. A lady met me and asked if I could help her. I was tremendously pleased. At last I had found something to do! She showed me a room that I could have for myself and promised me three meals a day. All I would have to do is make myself available to the men of the bar as a prostitute. There was no choice, so this became my way of life; and it has gone on for years.

"But today the saddest thing of all has happened. A man came in. After a while he noticed that I had only one good arm and the other was artificial. He burst out in hatred against me, almost spit in my face, and ran from the room. I cursed him in return and started to weep. Big tears were streaming down my face. Deep down I had been crying all the time, now I could no longer restrain it. It struck me plainly that even the lowest element in all society was reviled by me. I knew that people of repute, with high standards, those who were leaders, had no use for me. Now it was clear that even the worst thought that I was worse still.

"A few hours later I recovered my composure a bit and turned on my radio. Nothing seemed to satisfy so I kept moving the dial until I came to station HLKY. Your program was on the air. You called it 'Sunshine for Youth Hour' because you wanted to emphasize that your message was one of hope. You had something that would change a shadow into sunshine. As I listened, I did not want to curse society and my nation and soldiers and men anymore. But I felt a strong urge to get out of here. I realized that I was living the life of an animal.

"Don't tell me, 'O you poor girl.' I don't want that kind of compassion. I've heard that from many places before, I am just too needy for that kind of sweetness. I'm too hardened right now to respond to any kindness. But I do want to accept Christ. You said Christ is the answer for everything. Is He really? Please save me. I have never needed help so much in all my needy life before. I don't even need a father and mother, a husband and children, a home of my own, as much as I need Jesus Christ who can forgive my sins and heal my life."

That is the kind of cry from the heart that God hears and answers immediately. He looks on the inward appearance and he saw that day a person longing for Him. He reached down and made her thoroughly clean. Once she was fresh and new within, it went to all of her body, to the outside as well. And

she became by the thrilling grace of God a trophy of the trans-
formation only He can bring. Christ had proved to be the answer as He promised.

§ "A JEWEL IN THE SLUM" (August 1959)

Jesus Christ came down from mansions above into a stable.
From the heights He condescended to live with men—the worst
of men. Because He wanted everyone to know the good news
of salvation, He was willing to live next to them and share the
Gospel personally.

This beloved example of our Saviour is the motivation I needed
constantly to continue my work with the underprivileged. It was
wearying to live continually in the mire of filth and human sin.
And so I always thrilled to see our Master working the same way
in the lives of others. Their willingness to reach the least because
of Him was a genuine inspiration to me. One such humble ser-
vant of God who impressed and encouraged me a great deal was
Miss Sunnie Choi.

Miss Choi was a wealthy person. Her early life was spent in
luxury and prominence. She was elite socially, well-educated,
with all the pleasures Korean life can offer. With her interest in
education and the good things of life she became a teacher in
a primary school.

During the war she wanted to become a welfare worker. Her
heart went out in pity to the many homeless children. Because
of this interest, she went back to school and trained as a nurse.
Upon graduation, this high-class lady became the director of a
Korean orphanage.

But God wanted to use her for Himself. At some meeting in
Seoul she was converted by a tremendous Pentecostal experience.
Immediately she felt that God wanted her to work in the slum
area. Even the orphanage was not enough sacrifice.

Miss Choi, the born-again, committed child of God, began to
testify personally in the Han River slum area. Everyone in Korea
knows what a place of degradation that is. God had given her
a burden for the underprivileged that drove her to do anything
He asked. In fact, she felt that to be really effective she would
have to live every minute along the Han River. Miss Choi found
a cave there and made that her home.

When Mr. C. S. Kim, a young blind man, was released from

prison, she took care of him as an adopted son. Before long he was saved through her testimony. Together they would spend their days helping the people along the river. Many children could not go to school so they taught them stories from the Bible. They worked with the blind and orphans, helping them make protective walls and roofs from rice sacks and other bags.

I was greatly impressed as I saw her life of cross bearing. How much she was like Jesus. What a thrill to know redemption had meant so much to her. Hundreds accepted Christ because they saw Him living daily in her life.

§ "GO TO NINEVEH CITY" (April, 1960)

It is deep midnight—my golden time for meditation. The soul and mind and spirit seem to become one at this hour.

Today I visited an asylum for the blind on the edge of Seoul. I wanted to stay longer, but couldn't. The many demands of my church ministry shortened the available time.

But now as I write in my diary, I cannot remove from my mind the picture of these blind people. Some of them were simply wandering aimlessly around, stumbling over any obstacle in their path. One of those I met was cursing himself. He complained vehemently against life and society. No one liked him, he said; he had been abandoned to himself.

But there was one young man who was really happy. He was blind, but he was singing and laughing anyway. I asked him why. His answer was short, but it rang with joy, "I am a Christian."

Now I began to think: The only answer for all the hopeless and discouraged is the light of Jesus. All of these blind were getting the same care. The only thing that made a difference was salvation. And then the question comes: Who will go? Just as with Isaiah, God said: "Who will go for me?" The blind need Christ or they have nothing.

"But don't send me, Lord." My heart rebelled at the thought. I couldn't go. Ministering to the slum area was enough. "I don't have the capability. I don't have a clear vision." It was midnight anyhow, so I went off to bed. But I couldn't sleep well. I wonder why.

Just a few days later I had finished a revival conference at the Woogum Presbyterian Church and was on my way home. As I came near the blind asylum once again, I felt compelled to stop in. As we talked, Mr. Kim, the director, asked me to witness to them. My response was immediate: "I cannot minister to them now, but I will preach a five-day series here if you desire."

Shortly after I returned home, I was deeply troubled. Something inside was severely restraining me. How could I preach to them? I had eyes. How could I reach them since I did not really understand their needs? Well, God spoke to me once more: "Verily, as you have done it to the least of these, you have done it unto me." I knelt down in submission and God spoke again: "Feed these my lambs." God's leading was clear. I must go and preach to the blind!

Nothing really happened during the first few days of the Crusade. And then on the fifth day God began to work a miracle. Many blind were now starting to search and wonder. Some of them stayed up the whole night before the final meeting to fast and pray. I arose at 3:00 that morning to prepare for an early morning prayer meeting that was scheduled for 4:30. Then I discovered the group already kneeling and keeping the vigil. We decided to have a 3:00 service.

Director Kim was the first to come forward. He confessed his sin in humble repentance before God. He was a Christian, but he wanted to be really dedicated. Then another man, Mr. Chun, who had recently tried to hang himself, accepted Christ and shouted "Hallelujah." By 8:00 thirteen had decided for Christ and testified to others.

Mr. Lee was one of these thirteen. He stood up to tell everyone what had just happened to him. He said that he could not explain what salvation by grace was all about, so he would sing about it instead. The song, "Bright, Heavenly Light" poured from his lips and his soul. While he sang, many stood up and raised their hands to heaven. They could not see each other, but the glory of the song stirred each of their hearts to reach for the heavenly light. Two or three times Mr. Lee repeated the song. He just couldn't stop. The blind in the valley were seeing a light through the miraculous power of prayer!

This was the beginning of my work with the blind. By the exceptional grace of God, this Mr. Lee became a co-worker with me in our ministry to those who have only spiritual eyes to fix upon Jesus.

But it wasn't until some months later that this new direction was confirmed. It was on the last day of 1960. As the old year came to a climax, God brought to my memory the great things He had done. But tomorrow would mean another year. Would it be a time of sorrow and hopelessness or a year of tremendous victory once again for Him?

I felt the urge to make a big decision for the new year. So I went to church and knelt down. By the grace of God I resolved to make the next year the greatest in my life and the history of His kingdom. On my knees I made a firm commitment to make myself through Him an eye for the blind. I would include the blind in an active way as part of my life and ministry.

In the United States, most of the blind are supported by welfare. At least they are not ignored. In Korea, the only employment is usually fortune telling. There are over 100,000 blind with no one to show them the way! In the last judgment, Jesus will say: "Have you helped the least, the blind, the sick, the prisoners?" I promised to be on His side right now.

§ "A LETTER TO THE CHURCH" (December 1960)

I preached this morning to a church about the parable of the prodigal son from Luke 15. This world today is exactly like the wilderness where the prodigal lived after he had left home.

Why did he leave home? Obviously he made an error in judgment. He thought if he had his father's money he would really be great. How mistaken he turned out to be! He based his decision on the same selfish desire for freedom that Adam and Eve had in the garden. He thought that if he left home, he would be able to go on his own and live fully for himself—and in that way become happy.

And isn't that often the case with the church? It is almost Christmas day now and the thought comes home especially at this important time of the year. Isn't it a tragedy how much the church takes its treasure and goes out like the prodigal into the world at Christmas?

Some say it is holy night, a peaceful night. I say the opposite. I believe that God is jealous of Christmas because of the attention that is taken away from His Son, through commercialism. The streets are lighted with red and blue and every other color as well. You hear "Jingle Bells," and sing it yourself in a lighthearted way. And the teenagers are saying that they must have the best fun in their lives this Christmas. And there goes the church, offering its flowers, and religions, and customs, and pennies to the world. The church looks like a candy store giving away some of its sweets and gifts to make people happy. Now isn't that exactly like the prodigal son who carried his trinkets far from home? He did not leave home to carry with him the good things that he had learned, the high standards his father had taught, the real blessings he had received.

How should we celebrate Christmas as Christians? According to the New Testament: just as the manger did, so must we make room in our hearts for Jesus. Just as the star did, so must we bring others to Christ. As the wise men gave, so must we give our hearts and talents to Him. As the shepherds believed the angel's message, so must we believe that He is the Son of God. As Mary did, so must we worship Him and love Him. As the angel did, so must we praise God and rejoice with Him instead of practicing pagan Christmas traditions.

God would remind us that we must leave the comforts of the padded pews, and not take these comforts along. We must go out with the Gospel of Jesus. We must go to the poor and underprivileged as Christ did—to give Himself. We must not lose our first love and carry some substitute of inferior quality in its place.

Read the story of Peter and John in Acts 3. A man near the temple was begging for money. Their answer was powerful and exemplary: "Silver and gold have we none. Such as we have we give. In the name of Jesus, rise and walk." How concerned are we also simply to bear that name of Jesus to our fellow men? The only answer is Jesus Christ.

This evening as my mind travels across the world to the blind, beggars, orphans without birthdays, hospitals, prisoners without light, I pray that the walls of the church may fall down. I pray that the cold minds of Christians might change from head knowledge to a compelling trust of the heart. Jesus pushed away from the temple to live with publicans and sinners, to be with those who really needed Him. May we go there with Him as well.

RAG PICKER MINISTRY

Rag pickers (former beggars and gangsters) attempt to raise a few pennies by collecting and selling old rags.

10¢ lunch for rag pickers.

5

MY BETTER HALF

§ **"I EXCHANGE GIRL FRIENDS"** (August 1960)

Every able young man must serve in the army, so I did too. Praise the Lord, He gave me a great mission field even in military service. I was assigned to the chaplain's section.

There was one other chaplain who had much the same background and ideas as myself. He became my best friend. And he was a very eligible bachelor! Many girls wanted to marry him. He was a tremendously attractive fellow—filled with the Lord, intelligent, and his personality was one of the best.

As we served together, we started a countryside church for the officer's wives in the surrounding areas. We worked closely side by side, slept together, made mud bricks early in the morning for the building, went to work for the army at 8:00. We were just like twins, living exactly the same kind of life.

Jewel was a girl who grew up with me in the orphanage. She had become almost like a sister to me. I considered her my best girl and introduced her one day to Chaplain Shin. She had just graduated from a university in Arizona with a Master's degree and one month earlier had returned to Korea. That same afternoon he took me to meet his best girl, Kathy. When he escaped from the Northern Communists, he had stayed in her home. And he lived in the same area for a number of years. She had become like a sister to him.

In Korea, you would violate custom if you married someone who looks like your sister. If you know each other too well or live closely together in the same town, you may not marry each other. You must go somewhere else to find your partner. People from the same church do not even marry each other. Some consider it adultery, it seems. There is no good reason, but this custom grew up through Confucianism.

Both meetings were really good. The fellowship was great. So we two bachelors returned rejoicing to the military camp. We spent the whole evening until two or three in the morning talking about these girls. I wanted to know all about Kathy, and he wanted to know all about Jewel.

Next morning I stole some of the government's time and wrote a long letter to Kathy.

§ "FORGET ME, PLEASE" (December 1961)

Chaplain Shin and Jewel moved swiftly. They wrote continually and had many dates. I became jealous. Everything seemed to be going very well for them. They had hit it off beautifully right from the start.

Meanwhile I tried hard to get my romance with Kathy off the ground. We wrote each other once in a while, but did not have enough dates (at least to suit me).

Then one day I received a letter from Kathy asking about my future. So I explained proudly that God had called me to be an evangelist. In my young Christian life I had all kinds of zeal, and perhaps not enough self-control. I explained all the details of my Christian faith and commitment to Him. I told her that I wanted to be an evangelist for all Asia, going from town to town.

A few days later I had my reply. "Forget me, please," she wrote. She admitted she didn't have enough faith to be an evangelist's wife. Maybe enough for a pastor in a local church, but that would be the limit for sure.

I didn't know what to do. I was tempted to write her: "Kathy, I am very willing to change." But my pride was much in the way. For some days I struggled deeply with the problem. Finally Chaplain Shin and I had a long discussion together. He promised he would convince her for me, so he took off on a trip to her home 190 miles away.

While he was there, he arranged a Sunday school teachers' dedication service in her church. I was to be the speaker. At my young age I didn't have much confidence in my speaking ability, but he felt that I could handle an audience. Since she was the vice-principal of the Sunday school teachers, this was a sure way to win her heart.

Well, I was there for the meeting. Somehow it went all right, but I didn't feel normal. It wasn't a sermon, but an address at which I did my best. Right after the meeting, I hurried to the back door. I noticed Kathy was trying to sneak out another way. Finally I apprehended her and said: "Kathy, you aren't my enemy, are you? Why can't I come over and talk with you tomorrow morning at ten o'clock?"

Her excuse was simple: "Tomorrow I have to go to school to teach."

I persisted: "I will see you at school tomorrow." And with that we said good-by.

Four months later we were engaged. Before long it was the day of the wedding.

§ "THREE PROMISES EACH" (May 1962)

After months of companionship in marriage we understood each other quite well. It was no longer possible to hide our weaknesses nor make excuses for our little failures. Then it was one day that we really wanted to be "a better half." We had talked about that many times, but now we wished to be serious about the word "better."

I solemnly promised three things. I had the habit of speaking and preaching for too long a time. So I vowed to pay Kathy one hundred won (the price of a good dinner) for every minute over twenty-five. Faithfully she watched the time when she was along. And I did too! But when she wasn't there, the temptation to go on for thirty or forty minutes was more than I could resist. You can guess what happened then.

I also promised to pay one hundred won every time I used the word "never" (Chuldarho). Kathy said that I was too dogmatic, made judgments too quickly, got too excited. It took only three or four "nevers" before I was cured. One hundred won is just too much money in Korea.

The demands of my work often caused problems and resulted in a third promise: I would be home no later than 11:00 at night. It often meant speeding across town with my motorcycle, but usually I keep the vow yet today. When I am traveling away from home, this vow is altered to say that I must write every day or pay up. Only once has this been violated.

Kathy responded with three similar promises. Our two boys

were basically her responsibility so she wanted to be the best possible steward of these sons of God. If she ever slapped John and Paul unnecessarily or without giving them a fair chance, she had to pay one hundred won. This simple promise meant an amazing amount of patience, but it is demanded by love.

Kathy also promised to handle the finances. For a year or so this had been a problem of concern. She was overly worried. So finally I pledged to raise the money, but she would have to organize it without ever mentioning the fact. Ten percent was set aside for tithing. Of the ninety percent left, nine percent was designated for elders—older people we knew who did not have family or children. Eight percent of the remaining eighty percent was reserved for transportation in the Lord's business. A little more than seventy percent was left to handle all the other expenses. And I testify that this is the way to live. We have had no financial problems whatever. Once I had to teach mathematics for a school term, but never have we encountered any difficulties as we move out in faith. I don't believe in the tithe under law. But I do believe ten percent belongs to God and I wanted to make a method for myself which I knew would honor God and overcome my human nature.

The third promise hinged on one that I had made: Kathy might not go off to bed until 11:00 at night. It was a simple thing, but it has meant a great deal in our home life. Never have I come home to a dark and uninviting house and family.

Every year these noble ambitions are reviewed and re-evaluated. If we are married, we are duty bound to be a better half so that together we can be a better one. The Bible says that we must leave father and mother, so marriage must be in God's will.

Yet I cannot forget the clear truth that God and our faith are always first. During the war, as many escaped from North Korea, they could not depend on family. Only their faith could get them through. I have an uncle in North Korea today, but I don't know one thing about him. There is absolutely no contact between North and South Korea. Nothing—no visits or letters. In Germany at least they can visit at Christmas time. In all these things, too, Christ must have the pre-eminence. Relationships with families can be broken, but our tie with our Saviour is eternal.

It must also be emphasized that families can get in the way of 100 percent commitment. Some of the greatest missionaries in Korea have been bachelors or single ladies who have been totally serious about the great commission. In many ways Korea is outstanding spiritually in Asia. This country has sent missionaries to Pakistan, Cambodia, Formosa, Thailand—and other places where Americans are not particularly adaptable or acceptable. Many of these victorious leaders have been unmarried. They are all out for God. God has taken every moment of their lives for Himself.

6

LEAST OF THESE MY BRETHREN

§ **"TRUE LIGHT, JESUS"** (September 1961)

Early one morning I jumped out of bed because I heard some singing in the distance. Both the voice and the words of the song sounded familiar.

It was only about 4:00, but I dressed to leave the house. Our prayer meeting would start in about 45 minutes and I might as well get an early start.

I followed the sound of the voice and it led me toward the mountains. In the distance, I saw a man kneeling down, and heard him singing and testifying from his heart: "Thank You for this precious salvation. Thank You for the love I have known. Thank You, Lord, that I can see because I have the light of Thy salvation. Yes, You are the Light! Bless me, Lord, so that 100,000 blind in Korea may know the joy of life in Jesus." As I approached more closely, I recognized my good friend, Mr. K. C. Lee.

It reminded me of the things God had done in his life and the testimony I had heard from him not too many days before:

"Three months after I was born, I was blinded by some disease. Nobody really knows what it was. I have never seen anything in the world, even my dear mother. Nor will I ever be able to see. I have no idea of color or shape or light.

"But I have a real burden to express the happiness and rejoicing I feel on the inside. Of course, before I became a Christian, I had tried to kill myself several times. What a joy that now I have found the light of the world, Jesus Christ, as my personal Saviour.

"Until He returns, or until the end of my life, I want to testify in song. I want to use my voice to bring the true light to my people who are blinded physically and spiritually. During the daytime I want to copy braille tracts and during the evening I want to sing hallelujahs! (3,000 copies of tracts for the blind, done by hand, were made in one month by Mr. Lee).

"I was searching for light. Now I found the light right here in my heart. At one time I was foolish enough to think I could find it from the outside."

§ **"OUR BLIND EVANGELISM TEAM"** (January 1962)

One of the exciting and blessed fruits of our ministry is the blind children's evangelism team. About eight children, mostly girls, have dedicated their lives and voices to reaching others with the message of love they have found in Christ.

On a typical day we start out together—myself in the lead with each of the kids holding to each other's belt following on behind. They are only ten-year-olds, but they have always been cooperative and very industrious. And so in the morning they would spend their time making tracts for other blind people. How they love their blind fellow-citizens! Their hearts go out to other blind people in a real way.

In the afternoons they will sing and testify in prisons. God always uses them there in unusual ways. Even the hardest prisoners have their hearts melted. As the little choir sings, the prisoners are reminded of their own children at home. Even though they have eyes, the prisoners realize that their children are not as happy and secure. At one of our meetings, over 3,000 prisoners attended and 400 accepted Christ. A fancy professional choir could not have done as much. The radiant love of Jesus which shines on their faces and carries on in their voices is just too much to resist.

These underprivileged also reach the other underprivileged boys and girls. In youth meetings, at clubs, on the street corners, God is using them to bring many souls into His fold.

God is well pleased to use these blind children and other blind people in our ministries, even though life is extremely difficult for them. The blind are social outcasts in Korea. Customs can be a cursed thing in a country; and this is certainly true of the blind in our country. Everyone thinks that blind persons have been cursed by God. People spit in their face three times in succession to show their utter contempt for them. The blind suffer complete neglect. Their situation is similar to the lepers described in the Bible during the time of Jesus and earlier in the history of Israel. As the lepers were hated and had to sit outside the city, so it is with the blind in Korea today.

When the blind become Christians, they are really happy. Never before have they felt one shred of love and acceptance from other people. As the love of Christ fills their hearts and they are loved by fellow believers, they are overcome with joy.

Our program for them stresses the presentation of the gospel message, through our asylum Sunday school, for example. We also provide Braille literature for them and they work for us in grateful response, doing even menial tasks with amazing results.

§ "NO LONGER A COMMIE" (July 1962)

The prisons in Korea are a despicable, stinking mess. There is no resemblance to the excellent jails in the United States. For months at a time, the prisoners are never given a change of clothes, or water to wash their faces. No one is allowed to shave for fear he will cut his throat out of despair instead. Visiting by families and friends is allowed under no circumstances whatever.

These prisons are the loneliest and most discouraging places in the country. The neglect and mistreatment of inmates is almost a scandal, but it's true. No wonder, that as God gave us a burden for the least, He gave us a heavy burden for these least of all. Tens of thousands are dying in their sin and living each day with absolutely no hope. We thank God for a vision to include prisoners in our frontier ministry to humans in desperate need.

But how can prisoners be reached? Who could possibly understand them? God has answered our earnest searching through Mr. Kim. Praise God for Mr. Kim — prolific worker, enthusiast for Christ. He is outstanding proof that each kind should reach his kind. There is no more effective way to evangelize the world.

I include his testimony as a witness that God can use us in any circumstances, no matter what they happen to be:

"Everyone has read in his newspaper of the outrageous acts perpetrated by Communist guerrillas in various countries. Knowing these masters of evil, it is nearly impossible to believe that someone like them could be used by Jesus Christ Himself. But that's what happened! North Korean mountain guerrillas were the most notorious operators during the Communist invasion of South Korea, and I was one of their most vicious leaders.

"One is used to thinking that only the righteous are chosen to carry out the work of the Kingdom. But the fact that God can use the most depraved and unscrupulous soul residing in the Oriental world is a miracle of His grace. I am living proof of the fact that it can happen. It happened to me.

"As a daring North Korean guerrilla, I was so good at my job that I was made commander of the guerrillas. Together we amassed hundreds of murders of men and women from the Republic of South Korea. I took for myself a wife who was a captain in the North's forces. Together we performed our duties as officers in the Communist network with superb efficiency and unflinching devotion.

"Few of us remained alive after the major encounters with the combined forces of the United Nations and the Republic of South Korea. We retreated to the hills, and I was then put in charge of a detachment of spies which operated in and about enemy towns. Cunning as our actions were, we were captured. I was put into a prisoner of war camp in solitary confinement. There was nothing to do now, but await execution.

"By now I was the father of a six-month-old daughter. According to Korean law, she was allowed to be with my wife in her cell while she served her time in prison. I considered the fate of our daughter, who was soon to lose her father. For the first time, I had misgivings about my terrible conduct. Each day that I spent in my solitary dungeon seemed like ten years. Each hour was a personal hell. My mind constantly rehearsed bloody scenes from my past as I awaited word of my execution date.

"One day a gospel tract was slipped under the iron cell door. By whom or how I'll never know. How I hated this leaflet at first. But in the idleness of my endless days, I welcomed even this to have something to read and occupy my mind. I read it, and reread it. Time and again I went over it until it became so crumpled from my handling that the words were indistinguishable.

"On another occasion the gospel of John was miraculously slipped under my door. I read it so many times I committed it to memory. Through its message I learned of Jesus Christ. I learned the precious message of salvation. It explained that God had a plan of righteousness for everyone's life, even for wrecked lives such as mine. I learned that even I could share in His plan and attain eternal life by having faith in the Lord as Saviour.

"The manifestation of God's Word was made even more revealing one night when I had a vision of Christ. I don't know whether I was asleep or awake. But I do remember how plainly I saw the nail prints in His outstretched hands. I cried out, 'O Lord, forgive me, a murderer.' Tears streamed down my cheeks as I cried for the first time since I was a small child. My heart told me that I wanted to dedicate my life to Him, though short it would surely be.

"After Jesus appeared to me, I had an understanding of the gospel of John which I never had before. The Holy Spirit had blessed me with a higher plane of comprehension. I now spent every waking hour with the little gospel. It became my most prized possession.

"One day the jailer handed me an official looking paper. Syngman Rhee had been re-elected as South Korea's president. This paper informed me that my sentence of execution was changed to life imprisonment. Praise the Lord! After so many years of solitary confinement, I was able to come out of my dark hell-hole and was transferred to a different prison.

"How good it was to be with people again. How glorious to belong to God! In the jail I preached to my comrades at every opportunity. To God's glory, hundreds of incarcerated men were brought to a saving knowledge of Jesus inside those walls.

"Mr. Ben Song visited our prison when he brought a blind children's choir to sing for us. He preached afterwards and was so well received that he was able to establish an official evangelism program in the prison. He made me his official resident representative there. A great harvest has been reaped for the Lord behind these locked gates (over one hundred per year). To be one of His instruments has been a joy beyond telling.

"How well I know the meaning of the Lord's words: 'A prophet is not without honor, except in his own country and his own house' (Matthew 13:57). Although I was able to lead many to the Lord Jesus, I was never able to reach my wife. After she had served her sentence for six years, she was allowed to visit me in prison every month. Though I witnessed to her intensely, I wasn't able to get God's message to her heart.

"Naturally, my wife's salvation lay heavily on my heart. Having exhausted my own resources, I asked my benefactor, Ben

Song, to minister to my wife. He kindly visited her and witnessed to her regularly for days, weeks, months. His message became indwelled in her heart as well as her head. Praise Him, she is now a born-again person.

"After serving in prison for eleven years, I was released for being a model prisoner. Our daughter, too, has accepted the Lord into her heart and life. Our family is now reestablished and completely dedicated to Him.

"Although I am on probation, I continue in my service of Him to minister to those behind prison walls. I might be there as a prisoner myself, or I could have been executed long ago, were it not for His concern for me. I was a tool of the devil. I am now a humble vessel of God. By grace I was scooped up from a reprehensible existence, from the depths of degradation into His loving arms for all eternity."

§ **"I WANT TO GIVE ONE OF MY EYES"** (September 1962)

Mrs. C. Y. Song is no relative in the physical sense, but she is a dear mother to me in Christ. Largely through her influence and work, God has been able to expand our ministry to the least. We had begun with the beggar boys and all the underprivileged of the slum area. But my special interest in orphans had not materialized into an effective program until close cooperation was developed with Mrs. Song. In spite of the orphanages which were raised up, thousands of children still remain homeless because of the devastation of the war. God laid this burden on a compassionate woman's heart—Mrs. C. Y. Song.

Mrs. Song was of Korean extraction although she was raised in the United States. Soon after her marriage, Mrs. Song was left alone with two sons, whom she taught carefully the faith of the Lord Jesus Christ. She walked with her Lord every day as He had become the Lord of her life early in her childhood. Her sons became boys in Christ as they were shown by their devout mother the ways of the Christian faith.

The blackest day of Mrs. Song's life occurred when one of her sons was killed in an accident. Naturally she became very discouraged with life because of her loss. God had taken away another loved one from her intimate family. But God, in His omnipotence, broke through her depression. He laid a burden on her heart for the orphans of Korea. She had read many reports from her homeland, and talked to many of the thousands of children in need.

Mrs. Song prayed incessantly for these children whom God had brought into her mind and heart. Her burden for them grew heavier as she prayed much about the situation. Finally she felt she should go to Korea to see the conditions there for herself. She asked God to make this possible for her. In His time, He did work out all the details: money, passport, and visa for her trip. It meant that she would have to leave her only son. He had finished college and graduated from law school. Now he was a senator from the state of California and could not leave his important responsibility.

But it was a happy day when Mrs. Song set foot on Korean soil. God had made possible her dearest dream—though she was now over sixty years old. Almost immediately after her arrival, she visited an orphanage. What a shock to see the incredible overcrowding. Young beggar boys had to resort to crime to provide even their scarcest needs. Hundreds of babies were dying because their mothers did not know how to use the unprocessed milk provided for their babies. Mrs. Song's background in the United States provided her with this knowledge. Scores of babies' lives were saved as she shared this one skill alone with the housewives.

But simply working in other orphanages was not good enough for her. Her real efforts in establishing an orphanage herself began when she found three cold and hungry little beggar boys trying to survive under a bridge. She insisted that they come with her though she was not sure where she would take them. She had no funds to provide for their care, but she could not ignore the voice in her heart telling her to take care of these little urchins. With her three charges trailing behind, she set out for the countryside.

In a spot by themselves, they began building a small room from mud brick. Here the four of them ate, slept, worked, and played. The structure was barely four walls and a roof. What a far cry from the affluent life she had enjoyed in California. But her love for the boys surpassed any of her fleeting thoughts of material things. She nearly forgot the comforts of a modern home. Just to provide for her boys was her concern. And even these poorly constructed four walls seemed luxurious to these little fellows who had been existing under a bridge without any shelter at all. Their happiness with the home, and her thoughts of Jesus' humble home, consoled her heart.

As time passed, she was able to add a kitchen. Later, with the boys' help she gradually added bedrooms made from mud brick to the original "all-purpose room." More and more boys found their way to Mrs. Song's care, and it became apparent she must have larger quarters to house them all. But how? This posed serious problems. She had no outside support.

But all of her needs had been met before by faith and prayer. Again, God provided by supplying a small farm for the work to be carried on. In return for his care, each boy did a share of the work. Each had schooling, and each was personally given his spiritual education by Mrs. Song. She saw to it that each of "her boys" knew the Lord and His teachings. It was a happy relationship, although full of endless tasks and responsibilities. But Mrs. Song loved her work and counted it a real privilege to serve these children.

Her material needs were always supplied in miraculous ways. Still, there were many instances of heartbreak for Mrs. Song. One morning she awoke to find that one of the boys had stolen everything of value: cameras, clocks, food, equipment, and money. During the night he had sneaked away with everything. With no food and her only money gone, she was at a loss to know what to do. She went to the mountains to fast and made supplication to God as she had on other occasions when seemingly unsurmountable problems had arisen.

She did not pray for the return of the tangible goods, however. She pleaded with God for the return of her boy and for God to make his heart right again. When she came home, an officer was waiting to inform her that the boy had been apprehended. He was being held in jail, waiting for her to press charges. Hearing that the boy was safe, Mrs. Song's heart was filled with joy. Her boy was found! She hurried to the police station, threw her arms around the boy and hugged and kissed him soundly. Her boy was back!

Later she pleaded with the judge to let the boy come "home" with her. She promised to be responsible to the court for the boy's future conduct. Tears filled her eyes as he was permitted to return with her. Since that experience, this boy has become one of the most devoted and fine young men ever to come out of a Korean orphanage.

Mrs. Song also wished to give one of her eyes to a blind boy whom she took into her walls. This boy had memorized over 2,000 verses from the Bible, and showed such strong promise that Mrs. Song earnestly desired for him to be able to see. But the boy refused her offer. "God is able to use me as I am," the boy reasoned. "If I became able to see, it might distract from the abilities God has given and the way He wants to use me. When I am weak, then I am strong." Mrs. Song continued to try to convince the boy. "I am old and can get along with one eye for the rest of my life. But you are so young and have so many years ahead that you could use the eye." He still refused her kind offer, because he believed that God had some purpose for his blindness.

Here is a woman who is living to give not only her life, but also her home, and her food, and even her eyes to the least of these, His brethren. How much do we really care about total dedication? Are we willing to give a tithe of our time or of ourselves? That may even seem too much. Mrs. Song has been willing to give up everything to answer the challenge of Christ that we take up the cross daily and follow Him.

Love means that kind of sacrifice. Love is not a theory or a theology or a moral code. The love of Jesus is a reality that changed lives. We can no longer just say, "I love You," but at every point we must live it, even to the extent of giving up our eyes.

§ **"KIM WITHOUT A BIRTHDAY"** (December 1962)

I have just finished reading the book by S. P. Kim, *A Boy Without a Birthday*. This is one volume that means much to us in Korea for it tells the story of thousands just like Kim.

Mr. Kim and I grew up in the orphanage together. He worked hard too. As he writes he describes the biggest heartache he had: No birth certificate and no citizenship papers. The only thing he knew was that he was born, and that he was a Korean, and that he had a name. For the rest, he felt totally cut off and alone.

After he grew up, Mr. Kim wanted to help the boys and girls in the orphanage since he understood their plight so well. He is now one of the counselors among the beggar boys in Korea. He works in the orphanage, too, and loves the children there even more than his own life. His great joy now is to tell everyone that they actually do have a citizenship — in heaven, since they are born of the Spirit. This message has made him one of the outstanding workers among the underprivileged.

Today in Korea, the buildings look more beautiful than they did before the war. The bridges and the roads which were destroyed were rebuilt again very soon. In terms of its physical condition, most of Korea has been restored. To most observers things look all right, at least vastly improved.

But this cannot hide the hurts that men carry around in their souls, even fifteen years later. Most may be well clothed by now, but in their hearts the pain is still acute. The orphans and the poor and maimed are still deeply hurt. Many of them carry the same burden as Mr. Kim: They feel they have no citizenship here. They don't know where they came from, and deep down they're even less sure of where they're going. It might seem strange that a name and a birth certificate could mean more than wealth and external comforts.

This is not restricted to the country of Korea, of course. In fact, as I think about divorce and remarriage in the United States, I wonder whether the same situation does not obtain. A person who is remarried may look happy and contented on the surface. Her new home may be the best she has ever had.

Yet all of these surface matters do not hide the problems that go on within. Children may be seared for life in their heart. Adults are often struck with a guilty conscience and uneasiness. Put a nail into a living tree and the scar is there forever.

MINISTRY TO THE BLIND

He dedicated himself to the Lord, receiving a great burden for the blind.

Blind K. C. Lee was saved in 1961.

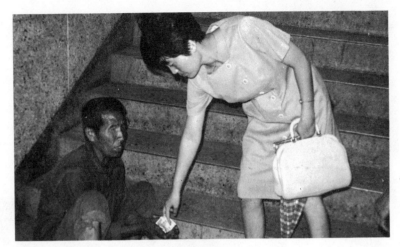

Most blind are outcasts in Korea.

Speaker and singer
on the road to
the blind asylum
for a meeting.

Blind girls led to meeting by young Christian worker.

Making braille tracts.

Here are our blind evangelist K. C. Lee and his new bride Jongja. "I will be your eyes."

Charles Lee, Ben Song, and C. Y. Kim,
former Communist Commander
saved while in prison now serving
in prison evangelism.

One of our prison campaigns.

Fruit for eternity.

Prison Bible Study led by George S. Song (Ben's brother).

Chapel Hour at prostitute rehabilitation center.

Juvenile delinquent boys spell-bound by Gospel message.

HARVESTING THROUGH ALL ASIA EVANGELISTIC ASSOCIATION

§ "SOMEONE STOLE MY CHURCH" (February 1963)

As our work grew and prospered in the slum areas, the matter of buildings took on some urgency. We did not want to limit the progress God was giving by bogging down in building programs. However, we did not want to hinder our growth by having no facilities at all.

The obvious solution was some kind of tent. It went up in a matter of hours and accomplished all we could hope for in a building. Every morning at 4:30 a faithful group gathered for the daybreak prayer meeting. Sometimes in the winters in the early morning the temperature dropped from five to ten degrees below zero and the tent was unheated. But they came anyway. Prayer played an extremely vital role.

About twenty days after the tent was set up, I came one morning at 4:20 for the prayer meeting. But there was no tent! Our building was gone. The people arrived and said: "Brother Song, where's our church?" I had to confess I didn't know. Someone must have stolen it.

We knelt down on the cold, open ground and had our prayer meeting. About six o'clock I went into the city to see if I could locate the person who had run off with our church. Then I saw a man on a bicycle heavily loaded down. It was my church! I ran up to him and he recognized me as the owner. He jumped off his bike and ran away. I had the church back and a bicycle as well!

From then on we had to stand guard during the night so the robbery would not happen again. This was especially hard during the long, cold winter nights. Every part of our bodies seemed to freeze solid—first our nose and face and then right on through our gloves and clothes.

One morning as I stood vigil, about three o'clock, a group came and said: "Mr. Song, aren't we going to have a prayer meeting today?" "At this hour?" I asked. "Why don't you wait until the regular time at 4:30?" The spokesman for the group stumbled through an apology. "I'm so sorry, but we just don't have any watches or clocks down in our village and we got up for the morning prayer meeting when the rooster crowed. We have walked five miles today to attend."

God Himself was with us as we gathered for a service which continued until six o'clock in the morning. Here was a body of people who met together, completely disregarding the time of day or their own physical health. They had not met together because the rest of the world had heard about the early morning prayer meeting and there was social pressure to continue it. They had no reason at all to carry it on as a pretense. That little congregation knew nothing about the rest of the world, nor even the rest of the city. But they did know one thing for sure: There were some things that can be accomplished only by prayer. They had discovered there is no other way.

Next Spring we began to build a more permanent structure. Every member brought mud bricks. The Sunday school children helped to make the bricks with their own hands. And when the great bricks had dried, they weighed an average of 30 pounds. The women of the church carried them on their heads to the foundation site and the men of the church laid those bricks, one upon the other, until the four walls were erected. Then the crude rafters were set up and the rice straw thatch roof was laid, sixty-eight feet long and forty-three feet wide. Through prayers, tears, nights of toil, sore backs and hands, a church building was erected to the glory of God.

Praise God, 120 faithfully attend the prayer meeting each morning. Five hundred attend the Sunday morning service. The one building has grown into five different ones in South Korea through this one church's ministry. Now I know God has answered our prayers when someone stole our church. It can never be taken again. The building is too solid, and it just has too much powerful prayer behind it.

This reminds me of the churches that are being stolen around the world today. How about it? Is yours being stolen too? Has not humanism, materialism, liberalism, formalism wrought havoc in America and elsewhere? This kind of robbery is a million times worse. We still had the people, so really we had kept the church all the time. A few walls we loosely call "the church" had been taken, but that's all. The church had only been carried to another city. What a tragedy when the church is carried off to hell instead.

§ "REVIVAL FLAMES" (July 1963)

I was invited by the Yan Pyong Presbyterian Church for a five-day revival meeting. This church is located only thirty miles from Seoul, but it took me seven hours to get there! The road was terrible and the bus was in even worse shape. I ended up walking over two miles as well.

The first night nothing happened. The church was really cold. The second night I asked them to stay with me in prayer throughout the night. Many of them, the young teenagers too, stayed. This brought revival sparks which began flaming the third night.

I began to preach about being honest before the Lord and being born again. During the meeting one young lady, in tears, accepted Christ. I'll never forget how happy she was. She came to the front and said: "Sir, I want to accept Christ." From her new heart she then gave her testimony to the crowd. This testimony was another spark. God began pouring out His Spirit upon the people.

A little while later, a middle-aged lady fell down on the floor. No one seemed to know the reason. From the front I noticed that her daughter had begun to cry. Then the group clustered around her seemed to think that she was dead. There was no breath, no pulse. Relatives and some of her friends heard about it and came in. One of the deacons called a doctor and a policeman to prove that she was dead.

I'm not sure what prompted me to do it, but I asked them: "Don't you believe that God could bring her to life?" I slipped through the crowd and went up to her body. I knelt down and began to pray loudly. Then everyone in that meeting began to pray loudly to God. Still there was no sign of life. How discouraging that was. Yet I believed that a real revival was just beginning. I prayed that God would use this situation to work in the hearts of the people. It made me feel uncertain. If our prayers were not answered, I would surely have to leave town because people would lose confidence in me and would not listen to any sermons.

But the other part of my heart said: "Why don't you trust God? All circumstances belong to Him." By faith, once again I cried out to God, "Lord, please answer our prayer." And then, just as the town councilman walked in, the lady opened her eyes and stood up. The first thing she said was: "I am a sinner. For twenty-five years I have not been completely honest in confessing everything to God." Then she began to confess all her sins and presented her testimony to the people. Just as she finished, she crumpled up again.

They gave her some water and she revived. Three of the deacons brought her to the pastor's home until she fully recovered. During the rest of the meeting, until 3:00 a.m., 178 accepted Christ. We didn't realize it was that late. So many came forward to repent and believe that we couldn't stop any sooner.

The aged father of the lady who had seemingly "died" had never come to a meeting before. But he stayed after coming to help. Finally he came forward and accepted Christ, too, as his daughter prayed. This man was a typical, stubborn, stumbling block to many. Many people were thrilled that his heart should melt in such a remarkable way.

I do not know whether she was physically dead or not. Her heart was not alive for sure, but as the Word of God went to her heart she was brought to life. Because of God's power which was manifested before their eyes they listened to the Gospel and believed and many were saved. What I thought would be a hindrance to the success of this revival meeting, God used for His purpose. We know that all things work together for good to them that love God.

That night I was really tired so I went to bed. But the people were not going home. Why? Because they wanted to stay for prayer. They all craved a deeper spiritual experience with the Lord.

The next evening, as early as 5:30 and 6:00, people began to come. We hadn't even rung the bell for the meetings which usually started at 7:00. Many lame and sick people came. Some were riding in a wagon, others were being carried, and many were unable to walk by themselves. They sat waiting patiently for an hour.

I had no experience with this kind of thing. But when I arrived I explained to them what a personal relationship with God is all about. I told them that God is love and does not want anyone to be sick, yet He sometimes uses sickness for His glory. Disease did come from Satan. It's an evil thing, but God can still use it so that His will is done. So I told them that I would be glad to pray for the people, but I didn't want to be a healer between God and man.

I knew that God can touch the body by faith. But I wanted to correct some faulty thinking, so I asked them: "Do you believe God is alive and that a living God can heal?" They shouted, "Amen!" "Why don't you pray for yourself, then?" I asked. "Touch yourself and in faith you can be healed."

So we prayed for five minutes. "If you believe and trust that you are healed by God's power, stand up." No one stood up. I began to preach about salvation. When finished, I told them if they wanted to pray with me about healing, they should stay. Many responded. Together we sang, read the Scriptures, and prayed again.

I knew I didn't want to stand between Christ and the people. Faith is a very personal thing. God alone can accomplish the wonders. They were beginning to worship me instead of God. So I left.

My partner, the blind Mr. Yuen, took over the final meetings on the fifth day. After that, there was just a tremendous revival. As we walked out into the streets after supper, we heard singing and devotions in the homes. Many nights of the week, teenage groups or missionary societies stayed up all night to pray. The morning groups were packed. The church grew so much that they had to begin another church not far away. The whole town was turned upside down.

I renewed my commitment to God to win souls and not be sidetracked into externals or the trappings of religion.

§ "BEST YEAR YET FOR HARVEST" (Fall 1966)

After several years God really began giving us a fruitful ministry. The number of duties mounted. There were thousands of demands on my schedule. I traveled in the fastest possible way from town to town and from city to countryside promoting the Gospel of Jesus Christ. But all I had was a bicycle. What a blessing to receive a motorcycle one day from Tom Woehl, the youngest son of my sponsors in the United States. It made a tremendous difference in time. God used it to multiply my ministry.

Everywhere people seemed more hungry for the Gospel than we could fill the need. Preaching, lectures, seminars, Bible classes, worship services, special meetings were opened to us. Youth clubs by the hundreds were asking for help. I was deeply involved in prisons, homes, churches, hospitals, open-air meetings, tents, buildings of every sort. Across South Korea, hearts were eagerly begging to hear more of the Good News of new life in Him.

We would set up large meetings in a town in the evening, and the results would flood out for hours afterward. In many places the people would respond, spending the entire night in prayer and thanksgiving. One night on my way to another city after late meetings, I stopped my motorcycle beside the road and prayed: "Lord, I am thrilled by the long prayer vigil of all these devoted people. Teach me to spend time in quiet meditation too. Help me not to forget close communion with You." I had been eating and sleeping and living intimately with the Lord. But I was grateful for this moment of rededication to a full prayer life with Him.

We can become so very busy in our service for Him that we forget the most important part of our Christian walk.

First and foremost, for a victorious Christian life, is our relationship *to God*. We will be in right relationship when we love God with all of our mind, soul, body and strength.

Second is our walk *with God*. This is fellowship with Him. We cannot have this fellowship until we first love Him completely and constantly. Out of this abundant, exciting life will come total commitment.

Third is our *service for God*. True, faith without works is dead. But works without love and constant fellowship with God is empty.

In spite of a hurried, minute-by-minute race with the clock, I still felt a heavy burden that we were not reaching enough people with the message of salvation in the cross. Were there additional ways that God could use us? Could there possibly be some other ministry that would reach thousands more?

One day I had a meeting with Rev. Robert Christopulos, a missionary in South Korea for T.E.A.M.* He explained to me his desire for a Seoul city-wide Youth Crusade. His idea was to bring sixteen American teenagers as a gospel music team from Forest Home, California. We discussed the ideas further. I spent time in meditation and prayer asking the Lord for guidance. Thus I was led to participate.

We organized a committee as the details developed. I was appointed program director. This gave me the responsibility for arranging all the details of the programs: speakers, music, radio and newspaper advertising. The Youth for Christ director in Seoul, Chaplain Oh, was given all the administrative details to handle. Rev. Ken Kremer, representative of Campus Crusade in Korea, agreed to take care of the follow-up and training of counselors. Over 200 were prepared for this important aspect of the Crusade. Mr. Jim Wilson, Far East Director of Youth for Christ, prepared a choir of 1,000 young people — 600 girls and 400 boys! This was accompanied by a 70-piece band.

By September 19 all the details were ready. One problem developed when we were informed that only six young people could come from America instead of the original sixteen. So we had to form a team of talented and spiritually-minded young Koreans. We had scheduled meetings every afternoon in a number of high schools around Seoul and we needed these witnessing teams. We were thrilled, too, that in God's providence a musical team arrived from South America just at the time we needed their help so badly. They were glad and willing to cooperate in the Crusade. God never makes mistakes.

"And we know that all things work together for good to them that love God, to them who are the called according to His purpose" (Romans 8:28). This only goes to prove what I've always said, that we Christians never have problems, just situations.

This was the largest Youth Crusade in the history of Korea. In Korea so much attention and respect are paid to adults that young people are virtually forgotten. Imagine how we praised God that over 70,000 gathered in five evenings on the dirty football field of Bae Jae High School. We passed out newspapers for them to sit on, but that's all.

Twenty-four hundred young souls came forward to accept

* The Evangelical Alliance Mission.

Christ. What a blessed harvest! Even one soul is worth more than all the money in the world, and God gave us 2400! The Bible says, that the angels rejoice over one soul that repents and believes. How wonderful their rejoicing must have been as God gave the fruits in this Crusade.

We conducted follow-up training classes for these young Christians for the next five days. Here we carefully explained the four spiritual laws, the keys for young people in understanding salvation. The counselors were thrilled and happy to tell these young men and women how the grace of God had brought them new life. Each one of the trainees was further developed in the faith by a Bible Correspondence Course.

The response from the city was so tremendous we knew we could not stop there. So we picked out four of the largest churches in the north, south, east, and west parts of the city. Thus we were eager to reach even more of the four million people of Seoul. We arranged four speakers and four music teams. Each night they rotated, and brought the message in the power of the Spirit to the lost and the least of Seoul.

The revival fire sprang out from Seoul to another five cities. Two teams were set up, one moving southeast and the other southwest. For a month the meetings continued in five major cities. Many thousands are now rejoicing in the Lord because of this ministry. Through these rallies was established yearly soul-winning campaigns throughout the country.

Tent churches go up in a few hours. God gave us this practical solution for our ministry.

Slum area tent church.

Early morning prayer meeting. One day
our tent was stolen.

Because the tent church was stolen, the people decided to work
hard, making mud bricks to build their own strong church.

This congregation is now also building a strong church of believers.

Five years later a new building, 500 average attendance at Sunday morning service, plus people meeting in the adjoining high school.

Every Saturday — Youth for Christ meeting.

A high school rally.

Small group training in Korea.

A meeting after grammar school.

A planning session with part of our staff.

We often start with an open air meeting.

We often hold meetings in local homes.

The next step is to let people build their own mud brick church.

Our rural ministry requires many hours of travel on trails such as these.

Calling people to church. This church is four hours' walk from nearest bus. My helper is my classmate Mr. You.

A fully developed countryside church where we had a campaign for the mining community.

Rural Director E. S. Hahn's church with land for potential conference training center in foreground.

One of our staff workers preaching the Good News—Mr. J. M. David in West Pakistan.

8

MY BENEFACTOR: THE UNITED STATES

§ **"LOS ANGELES INTERNATIONAL AIRPORT"** (October 1966)

After months of tremendous revivals, rallies and innumerable activities, I felt a keen need for rest and vacation. The city-wide crusades and revival meetings in Korea had been well received and CCI (Canaan Christian Institute) recommended me and sponsored a trip to the United States. I was terribly eager to visit my American sponsors and thank them. For fourteen years they had faithfully stood by me with ten dollars per month. It would also give me an opportunity to thank the people of America for the help they had given the needy of my land.

It was an exciting day when I landed at Los Angeles International Airport. But the happy meeting I had anticipated with my sponsors did not materialize. I had written a letter five days before, but my plane took only eighteen hours and my letter seven days! To make matters even worse, I left Korea at 3:00 on Saturday afternoon and arrived in Los Angeles 2:00 the same day. I learned later that they were also on vacation in Alabama. There I stood. No one had come to meet me, and I did not know one other person in the whole country.

Poor Ben Song had become an orphan once again. I walked around wondering what to do next. I had no plans and was not able to speak the language. But this orphan knew that he belonged to God and could ask Him. So I knelt down and prayed in the lobby of the airport: "Lord, here is Ben. I know You are the same God in Los Angeles as the One I knew in Korea. I'm trusting You to guide my way." At once a genuine peace came into my heart.

As I opened my eyes, the first people I saw were an Oriental couple. I approached them and explained my situation. He did not understand Korean too well, but he grasped my situation. Mr. Yim suggested: "Why don't you check the yellow pages and find a Korean church or embassy?" The yellow pages! I did not realize there could be so many addresses! Now if I have a situation, I always turn to the yellow pages for the answer.

Mr. Yim drove me to the Korean Baptist Church where I met Mr. Moon, a student who lives in a small apartment. That night I slept in his bed, but he had to sleep on the floor. I hated to push a man out of his bed, so I decided I must not stay any longer. I reaffirmed my conviction that He would guide me to do His bidding. I decided once again that by faith alone I would travel in this country and not actively seek help from anyone.

The next day was Sunday so Mr. Moon took me to his Sunday school where I spoke in Korean and tried out some English. After church I asked him to leave me at the Church of the Open Door in Los Angeles. There I met a lady who had visited me in Korea, having attended one of my meetings there. She invited me to her home in South Pasadena. I spoke to her women's group and my travels across the United States had begun.

You might wonder how I began giving a testimony in English. Well, a lady in Ventura sensed my problem a day or two after I had arrived in California so she helped me write something out in a notebook. For four or five days, I read it thirty or more times a day to memorize it. I included a testimony in song to help me get by. Within three weeks I was able to say my message freely, though conversation in English was still difficult for me.

The doors flew open across the state of California. Within the first couple of months I had covered fifty-four towns and cities and spoken at 112 meetings. God was blessing mightily—in Glendale, Burbank, Redondo Beach, Long Beach, Ventura, San Diego, Santa Barbara, Monterey, San Francisco, Santa Cruz and many more. When the Woehls returned home and read my letter, it took a bit of searching to find me! The Spirit was leading every step. I had traveled all these miles by the grace of God for only $9.35! Praise God that our God is a "yes" God. While we are trusting and depending on Him, He always answers "yes" to His children. We His children should answer "yes" to His command also. Total dependence on God is faith and independence is failure. We Christians never have problems, just situations. All the situations will turn to His glory through our faithfulness, prayers and patience. It happened.

§ **"MY PRIVATE BARBERS"** (November 1966)

That $9.35 included $2.50 for my first haircut in America. I went to the barber shop and I was shocked. After the barber had finished I asked him, "How much does it cost?"

"$2.50 please."

I said, "No! You're kidding me."

The barber came back, "No, I'm not. Where are you from?"

"From Seoul, Korea. And over there haircuts are only nineteen cents in the cities at the expensive places. In the countryside, they're ten cents or sometimes only nine cents."

It was his turn now: "No, you're kidding me."

Well, when a price is set in Korea we always negotiate. Sometimes as much as twenty or thirty percent is discounted from the original. So I began to whittle away at that astronomical figure. I didn't realize that this was unacceptable, though I noticed he was getting disgusted.

He finally lowered the cost to $2.00 since "I was a foreigner," as he put it. I paid, but with tears. In Korea, fifty cents will win one soul through our mission workers. $2.00 wasn't simply paper. It meant four souls to me.

Not many days after this horrible experience, I observed one man where I spent the night. He seemed to have a home style hair cut. So I asked him about it and he confided that his wife always cut his hair. *That's great,* I thought.

The next morning after he went to his business, I asked his wife: "Would you do me a favor?" She said, "Sure, what can I do for you?" When I asked her to cut my hair she was startled: "Me? I'm not a barber." I insisted she was and finally the truth of what her husband told me came out. "I'll just pay you $2.50 and you can go to the barber." "If I get $2.50," I said, "it goes right to Korea. Let me ask you once again. I trust you."

She was the first of thirty-three dear ladies to cut my hair. One night I was at the home of a former movie star, Marla English Sutherland in California. At the dinner table as I related some of my experiences, I learned that she cut hair too. The next morning she became seventeenth on the list.

§ "A PENNY OFFERING" (December 1966)

Today I had a really great offering—a penny! It was one of my first meetings and Mrs. Thelma Myers, wife of First Mate Bob from the Haven of Rest ministry, was in the audience. She came up to me afterward and placing a penny in my palm she said, "This is all I have right now, but it is yours for your ministry." Then the dear lady gave me some unforgettable advice: "Ben, may I advise you? Don't depend on money, but trust the Lord. But be careful of every cent you get."

Some time later I received a fifty dollar check from that kind lady whose advice was worth so much and which I took so seriously.

What is a faith mission? Does it mean begging for money? Of course not. The Bible says in effect: "Freely have you received the Gospel, freely must you give it away." If we are doing this, God will provide. We don't even have to ask for money. In our church in Korea, we do not pass a collection basket. We only have a dedication service once a week during the morning worship in which we sing the doxology and the deacons place the offering plates on the altar. As people are led during the week they can bring their gifts to God.

Once I was in a church in Korea in which they were raising money for a tent ministry in a rural area that had never heard the Gospel. I hated this method, but the church was doing it and I was the speaker. Though I wanted to leave, I knew I had to stay.

The chairman of the elders began to announce the goals and people raised their hands to pledge their contributions. Many people gave a sacrificial offering and each time the people responded by clapping. One fellow announced: "I will give so much." It was the largest of the day. There was a vigorous clapping in response.

One old lady raised her hand next. The first to arrive at the meeting, she had come in hobbling on her cane. She had spent the time in prayer asking for a blessing. Now she raised her hand. Everyone, including myself, was amazed. How could she possibly give anything? Well, she pledged a dime. The audience was absolutely quiet. No one clapped. I could not resist standing to my feet. Pointing to the cross I said: "Couldn't you see Jesus clapping with His nail-pierced hands?" Immediately the audience arose and really started to clap too. I knew then that the Spirit of God was moving. I asked the chairman if we could just pass an offering basket and allow the people to give as God led them. When we were finished, more than twice the goal had been collected.

I do not believe in tithes according to the law. God wants the one hundred percent commitment of the will as this lady showed. Everything we have belongs to God. All of this we must use as His will leads. God doesn't want our collection money, but our all.

In my travels and meetings I always share with others and never receive. While in my car one day, I was thirsty for spiritual food. So I turned on the radio. There was beautiful music ("His Name Is Wonderful") by a quartet. After the music, the speaker explained what faith was about. He used the phrase, "I believe," about nineteen times in fifteen minutes. But somehow that message didn't give me a blessing.

Why not? Just before closing he exclaimed that if his audience didn't send in at least 500 letters they would have to discontinue the program. "We don't have any denominational affiliation," he said; "we are a faith mission, and we are totally dependent on you."

That statement gave him away. I seriously wonder whether a faith mission has to beg that way and imply that their continuance depends on the listening audience. Faith is a reality. It is not a program or method—it is trusting. By faith we have already received. How then can it be a matter of whether we will receive? We have already received, so we must give. This is what a "faith mission" is all about. If we are really concerned about giving in love to others we need make no justification for ourselves.

§ **"STRANGE FOOD"** (December 1966)

There are many differences between Korean and American customs and language. American food, for example, is much different from Korean cooking, but I find most of it enjoyable.

Traveling "by faith" one is greatly blessed if he appreciates the food that is set before him.

However, there is one food I refrained from ordering: a hot dog. I could not imagine people eating such things even though I heard that they were one of America's favorite foods. I saw many signs that advertised the hot dog.

After a church meeting I went out with some others to a restaurant. Two of the people ordered hot dogs! I was really amazed. "You order hot dogs in a restaurant? You Americans are funny people indeed." A few minutes later I found out that a "hot dog" is not really a dog. This softened my shock. In some rural areas of Asia, when people are really desperate, they will eat dog. But America is a developed and educated country. I just could not imagine their eating dogs. I still have some reservations and have a strange feeling when I do order a hot dog now myself on occasion.

One day in Wisconsin we met after an evening meeting for some refreshments in a home. The host asked me if I would like a soft drink. "How about root beer?" My instant reply was, "No." When offered a coke I said that would be fine. The junior pastor ordered a coke with me, but the senior pastor ordered a root beer. And so in my mind there was a big question mark. What kind of church could this be? It seemed all right when I was there. How could the pastor do it? Wasn't he a conservative Baptist preacher?

I was even more surprised when he drank the root beer right down. In Korea, a Chinese doctor has devised a medicine from beer by combining it with roots and burying it in the ground for twenty days. This potion is the strongest liquor anywhere. And he was drinking root beer in one or two swallows!

The next morning I went to the lady of the house to ask her about it. I wanted to know. "Do you have some more root beer?" She said she did. "Do most pastors drink root beer in the States?" She said they did. I was terribly confused by now, but finally we got everything straightened out and had a good laugh over my misunderstanding.

When I was speaking at the North Long Beach Brethren Church, I learned something else about American customs. I was excited since this was the church supporting Mr. Ken Kremer who has been used of God in Korea in my personal salvation. It was a great meeting!

After the service I was invited to speak to the college students for the purpose of having discussions. The pastor told me that this group meets in private homes, therefore he had asked me to follow him. I was waiting for him in my car and I was watching for him to come out, when I saw a man wave at me as he got into his car. Thinking that it was the pastor, waving his hand up and down beckoning me to follow him, I jumped in my car and followed him. About five miles later, he arrived at home and drove the car right into the garage and I right behind him. I got out of my car and he said to me, "Mr. Song, why did you follow me?" I replied, "Didn't you wave at me up and down (which means, 'come on,' in Korea)?" His answer was, with a big smile, "Oh, I was waving good-by to you."

Then it dawned on me that motioning up and down in America means good-by. In Korea it means, "Come here." We say good-by with an underhanded gesture. Now you probably no longer wonder why I'm confused sometimes in your country.

And then there's my experience with the yellow light some years later, after I learned to drive. In my country, a yellow light means we must slow down and turn left. One day I saw a yellow light, slowed down from forty to twenty, but kept right on going. I was a little startled to see the light change to red, but it didn't worry me. A few moments later a policeman pulled up beside me and ordered me to stop. "The light was red. Why didn't you stop?"

"Sir," I said, "I slowed down. What's the difference between stopping and slowing down?" He was quick with his reply: "Eighteen dollars is the difference."

Well, that's a lot of money so I felt I had better testify to him to make it worthwhile. I took out one of my booklets and began explaining my life's story. At this point, he was a little irritated and said: "Let's get down to business."

He asked me for my address. "Which one?" I replied.

"You have more than one?"

"Yes," I said, "three. One address is in Korea, one in heaven, and one in the United States."

"I'll take the one in the U. S.," he retorted.

Since I was traveling, I gave him the location of the Korean embassy. Giving him that address involved a lot of red tape for him—including contact with the South Korean government. He finally let me go, since I was ignorant of this law as a foreigner and honest as a minister. By my testimony I had given a gospel ticket to him (a warning) for eternal life. In return I received a verbal warning about my physical life.

§ **"MY FIRST BIRTHDAY PARTY"** (February 1967)

My first really good party was on my birthday, February 22, 1967. My beloved sponsors, the Woehls, prepared this occasion for me. They invited me and all their relatives to come. We prepared a tape for my wife Kathy. There were many beautiful cards. They gave me a slide projector as a present and this was sent to Korea for the youth ministry there.

The Woehls are the family that supported me for fourteen years. Now they have pledged to take care of our family's living expenses —$40.00 per month. No wonder I want to show appreciation to them.

This is symbolic of the thousands of Americans who support Korean orphans. As they send in their gifts, they are not backing organizations as such, but they are helping needy persons. All of the orphans who have benefited in this way would like to say thank you, but cannot. I want to thank the United States for them. I am an example of how God can use a small investment of money and translate it into the saving of souls and bodies for His glorious kingdom.

§ **"POOR WIDOW KATHY"** (June 1967)

I have been away from home for a few months now in the United States. Today I received a letter from my dear wife, Kathy:

"It's midnight here in Seoul. How quiet and dark it seems. I feel especially lonely now.

"Undoubtedly you have just come back to Los Angeles from the Midwest. Of course, I will get all the information in your letter a few days from now. But tonight I am really wondering about you. I trust you are healthy and happy.

"I don't have any reason for sorrow and heartache; but I guess it's just like a teenage girl. Tonight I could not control my heart. I have wanted to cry all evening because of my weakness of faith. Or maybe because you are not here.

"A few days ago, John got a cold. Before he recovered, I caught the cold too. Maybe I really haven't gotten over it yet.

Perhaps you understand and realize my situation right now. Every morning when the boys wake up, they ask: 'Mom, we have slept another night. How many days now before dad comes back?' Today is the eighty-fourth day that they have asked the same question. I hope you come before the one hundredth!

"Outside in the yard today I heard their conversation with their friends: 'You know, my dad is coming back from the United States by airplane. We have turned over many calendars, but when we turn the next one he will be home.' Tonight they asked me to turn over two or three at one time so that time will hurry a bit. Sounds like John, doesn't it?

"A few weeks ago, we received a package from the Los Angeles Church for the blind at Bulkwangdon post office, box 4. I went to the blind asylum and Canaan orphanage and told them of the love of those in the United States. Tell this church how grateful the children and all of us are.

"One thing you ask me—whether you should stay or not. We began from nothing. God has honored us, and has given us everything we do have. So I am willing to trust this matter to Him, too. If the Lord leads you to stay, I will accept His will and gladly be patient. But really deep down in my heart, I want you to come back or for myself to join you in the United States. How nice it is to be one family. I never knew before you left how important it is to give love to someone. To receive it is wonderful, but we must give it as well.

"Now it is almost one o'clock in the morning. Excuse me just a minute as I go to check the chidren. They really look sweet. As I see them sleeping peacefully, these two boys are a real comfort for me. They give our life some real purpose and meaning. I just gave them a kiss and I realize again that a separated life is difficult. But don't worry. Really we are very happy.

"We have Jesus so we have everything. So we have to be careful. We must give every step over to Him. I know you are really dedicated to the Lord. But please care for yourself too! I worry about your socks and pants, etc. You are traveling in a great country. Americans are an educated people, so look your best.

"I love you and know you love me too.

"Good night."

This letter places a heavy burden on my mind. How much must an evangelist's wife sacrifice? Does she have to give up as

I must? What does going to Calvary's mountain mean for her? Should she have to deny herself the basic comforts of home and family? In my heart, I do not yet know the answer.

The same question is involved with the children. The minister's children are watched more carefully than any others. They must be held in strict obedience or others will criticize. What kind of discipline is right for a pastor's family? May they be neglected at all for the sake of the calling to preach the Gospel? Perhaps the reader has his own answers to these important questions.

Opportunity came to visit
the United States. Farewell
at Korean Airport.

Letter from Daddy eagerly received.

Home is the first church for the children.

9

SUITCASE MISSIONARY

§ **"SENT BY GOD AS A MISSIONARY"** (February 1967)

Because of my very broken English, it was difficult to speak a full thirty minutes, so I filled in with that beautiful hymn "Amazing Grace." Even though my English was hard to understand, hearts were moved.

After one of my morning services in the Los Angeles area, I was invited to lunch at the home of one of the deacons, a Mr. Gene Ross, along with friends of his. That evening I was to speak in Long Beach, but had no way to get there. The Lord provided transportation through my new-found friends at Mr. and Mrs. Ross's home, a Mr. and Mrs. R. I. Powers.

That evening they offered me a room in their home. The result of this fellowship provided me with much needed transportation in those early months in the United States. They drove me to most of my meetings. On the way, I was able to practice my English, for I was corrected constantly by Mr. Powers. Soon I was able to be understood and able to communicate much better.

Many churches gave me love offerings and honorariums. Up to this time it never occurred to me that God had sent me to this country as a missionary. I never thought that America would need missionaries, for more than ninety percent of the missionaries in Korea come from the United States. This told me that America was strong spiritually and I looked forward to coming here to perfect churches.

So the beginning of my tour was a shock. I spoke to a big church in Monterey Park, California, because they had been supporting Korean orphans for twelve years and never had heard one speak. When I finished, a lady came up to me and said: "That was the first time we have heard the Gospel in many, many years. We used to, but not anymore."

On Tuesday night I came back to this church, this time to a ladies' missionary meeting. Carefully I explained the way of salvation, using the blackboard for sketches and illustrations. Would you believe it? Out of 140 ladies in attendance, 43 responded when I presented the invitation to accept Christ. They were hungry for a true gospel message, they were thirsty for the living water of Jesus Christ. For the first time I saw the great need in American churches. I knew that if I traveled, I could say thank you for American compassion and help, and tell the American people too about the simple message of salvation.

It seemed that at every corner of the street there were abandoned young people. The Lord opened the doors for me to share my testimony with these American youth.

I came here to say thank you to America, but because of all these things that were happening, I came to realize that God had a definite purpose for sending me to this country other than just for a thank you tour. A definite sign was my receiving a permanent resident visa as the first Korean missionary to the U.S.A.

All things work together for good. After hearing Mrs. Powers' testimony of how she had prayed for leadership concerning fulltime missionary service, I knew that the Lord had a purpose in placing me in this home for a short time. Here we began answering much of the correspondence and began keeping records and sending receipts. It grew until today All Asia Evangelistic Association is a government recognized non-profit organization, with a devoted seven-member board of directors and a seven-member board of reference.

§ "OUT OF THE CONVENT TO CHRIST" (March 1967)

The Lord wonderfully blessed at one of my Sunday evening meetings at the North Chapel in Redondo Beach, California. We rejoiced all the way home and praised the Lord for all that He had done for us.

Sitting around the fireplace enjoying an evening snack, Mrs. Powers was prompted to tell me her testimony:

"It has been said many times that religion is man seeking God and that Christianity is God seeking man. I am reminded of the day that I purposed in my heart to enter a convent. There I could be closer to God than any other human being.

"Having been born and reared in a Roman Catholic family, it was perfectly natural to think of priests and nuns as supernatural beings. I was about eleven years old, when walking home from school one day with a close friend, we were discussing priests and nuns. After many pros and cons on the subject we decided that nuns were people just like everybody else. That became the moment of a great decision. From that time on, I knew I would become a nun! I counted the years, months, and weeks. The thought never left my mind. Of course, the nuns helped to keep the thought alive by assuring me that it was God calling me to this great vocation.

"It is not the intent and purpose of this testimony to go into detail concerning the training and the life behind cloistered walls. It is, however, my definite purpose to testify of how God dealt with my soul in spite of this indoctrination.

"In Hebrews 11:6 we read that He is a rewarder of them that diligently seek Him. I sought Him in every ritual but still I could say with the Psalmist: 'As the hart panteth after the water brooks, so panteth my soul after thee, O God.'

"One afternoon, having finished the duties assigned to me, I went into the chapel earlier than the other nuns. As I sat in that beautiful sun-drenched room, reciting the rosary and praying to Saint Theresa and to Saint Joseph, my eyes rested on the crucifix over the altar. As I gazed at the pathetic figure on the cross, for the first time in my life the question arose in my mind, Why did Christ have to suffer and die? I could not answer that question.

"In giving this testimony, while dealing with Roman Catholics, I usually pause here and ask them if they can answer that question. The majority cannot. Some say that He died for the sins of the world. But none can say that He died to save them. The emphasis in the teaching of the Catholic schools is on the baby Jesus and there He stays and is 'adored.' We have learned of His death as a historical fact. But emphasis is put on praying to His mother, the idea being that she would obtain favors for you from her Son more readily.

"Shortly after that, I began to take steps to leave the convent. Going back into the world was an unusual experience in

that it was some time after Pearl Harbor. I left a world of affluence and came back into a world where hardly anything could
be bought without coupons or stamps. I would not go back to
worship in a Roman Catholic Church; neither would I go into
a Protestant Church, because of our teaching that it was a sin.
I remember feeling very much like the man without a country.

"My path finally led to California where my husband and I
chanced to hear a minister who had been televising his services.
We went out of curiosity. The message that Sunday evening was
a beautiful word-picture of the crucifixion of Jesus Christ and
why He had to die. It was made very clear and I understood
that I was a lost sinner and that Christ came to seek and to
save those who are lost. 'He is not willing that any should perish
but that all should come to repentance.' The preacher explained
that it was not necessary to go through a priest in a confessional,
for we have one God and one Mediator between God and man,
the man Christ Jesus, and that He is the answer for our sins.

"I understood, praise the Lord. I believed, repented and confessed. He saved me. 'But as many as received him to them
gave he power to become the sons of God, even to them that
believe on his name.'

"Then I remembered, as I stood at the front of the church
with many who had come for salvation, the sun-drenched chapel
in the convent many years previous. At that time I had asked
the question: 'Why did Christ have to die?' I had the answer:
He died to save me.

"It's been several years since I found Jesus Christ as my personal Saviour. I have prayed for some time concerning full-time
service. How I thank Him for this great opportunity of serving
Him as secretary with the All Asia Evangelistic Association."

§ "THE MIDWEST TOUR" (April 1967)

Already I had received invitations from Chicago and Lincoln,
Nebraska, and they were asking for a tape of my testimony to
play before I arrived. I asked the Powers: "Do you have a
tape recorder?" They had a small one and I needed it badly.
Energetically I began to record some songs, a message, some in-
troductory words about myself and ministry.

About that time, Mr. Powers became very sick, and the family doctor, Dr. Frank Gaspar, was called to the home. He saw me laboring with tapes and the recorder and wondered what I was doing. I told him, "I'm making a tape for some future contacts." He wondered out loud how I could possibly send a tape like that and expect to make any kind of impression. "I have a great deal of recording equipment," he said. "It's one of my hobbies and I spend a great deal of time with it. I would be glad to help you out." He is a tremendously busy doctor, but later he came back with his machines and helped me until 2:00 a.m. in preparing a professional tape.

The next day he called up and asked me how many copies he should make from the master. I only had a few dollars in my pocket so I told him that two or three more would be enough. He was surprised that I didn't ask for a dozen, but said no more and hung up. Before long, he made another visit to our house. This time he presented me with twenty-four tapes, all expertly done, and he gave them to me for nothing. I was overwhelmed by the way God answered prayer. He proved again He is a "Yes" God for His children. My cup was running over. If we totally trust Him, He will respond!

I was now prepared to leave California. But Mr. Powers cautioned me and said: "You must have at least $200.00 in traveler's checks before you can go on a trip like that." My answer was simple and to the point: "Don't you think Chicago's God and Los Angeles' God are the same?" Anyway he gave me a $50.00 check.

Doors opened throughout Nevada, Arizona, Utah, and Colorado for numerous meetings. Many people gave me money for personal expenses but I never had occasion to use it. While in Denver, I received a letter from our Korean Orphanage Director about special needs for heater repairs. Taking stock of my personal fund, I found to my surprise that I had $216.00. The heater took $200.00 and $16.00 carried me hundreds of miles on my journey to Chicago, Wisconsin, Kansas, Nebraska, and then back to Colorado. All church offerings were sent directly to Korea through our headquarters in Ventura, California.

Living by faith and not by circumstances, one doesn't need to worry. According to His Word, all circumstances will work for His children. We cannot understand or run faith mission work by computers. We have to do our best through total dedication and He does the rest for us.

I went into the state of Arizona without a single contact. There were a few addresses in my suitcase that I had picked up from previous meetings, so I got on the phone and began to call. God opened doors in a tremendous way and before long there were more meetings than I could possibly handle.

One of these experiences was in a Mormon church. They heard a radio and television interview and saw the story in the newspaper, so a representative of the Mormon Social Service Department called. He wanted to know if I could come to talk about social work in Korea. He asked me if I were an LDS. LDS, LSD, I didn't know for sure what the letters meant. The caller explained, "Latter Day, do you believe in latter days?"

"Certainly, I do," I replied. "These are the last days before Jesus comes again."

"Good, do you believe in saints too?"

I thought that I was one of the saints, a child of God, so I answered again: "Sure, I do." So the meeting was opened for me.

After the meeting, two boys came to ask me: "Have you been anointed by the Bishop to receive the Holy Spirit?" "No," I said, and showed them Acts 2:38 from my Bible: "Repent, and be baptized every one of you in the name of Jesus Christ for the remission of sins, and ye shall receive the gift of the Holy Ghost." We discussed this for some time.

Some days later one came to me and told this story: "I went to the Bishop with these verses and your ideas. I asked how this poor Korean orphan could be filled with the Holy Spirit and not have been anointed by one of our Bishops. The Bishop admonished me not to listen to you. But I do want to know more." He is now a member of an evangelical church.

One of the many interesting encounters I had during this trip occurred when I spoke at a Wisconsin high school. The principal cautioned me that a reporter was waiting for me. He was incensed and wanted to know why a religious message was permitted to be made in a public school. In my speech, I had related that America has many religions, churches, schools, and all the material things it could want; but its greatest need is Christ.

After the meeting, the reporter invited me to a coffee shop. He asked my opinion about Vietnam, and about teenagers. Then after I had answered his questions, I began preaching Jesus to him. In my heart, I felt that his real intention for being there was a deep desire to know more about Jesus.

At first, he just listened politely. But as I continued I could tell the message was getting to his heart. When I asked him if he wanted to accept Jesus into his heart right then, he regained his composure and said, "Here? In this place? No, not here, but maybe in my church."

I asked, "Why?"

He said, "This is the wrong place. I have been a Roman Catholic for fifty-three years. I have to go to the church."

I replied, "Do you have to go to a funeral home in order to die? This is as good a place to accept Him as any."

He looked at me and shaking his head said, "Mister, you must be unbalanced."

"No, I'm not," I retorted. "Time is short. Today is what is important to your eternal life. Yesterday is a cancelled check. The past is written already. You can't change even a dime from a $1,000 cancelled check. Tomorrow is a promissory note. But today is cash in hand. Tomorrow belongs to God. Your salvation is a matter of today. Don't put it off until tomorrow. Our lives don't have any guarantee."

In a wave of realization, the reporter came to the Lord right there. He gave the meetings a favorable write-up in his paper. Not only that, he gave me a check for ten dollars to use in our Korean work.

# # #

Lincoln, Nebraska, gave me two special opportunities. I appeared on the Back to the Bible Chapel Hour program and had a chance to give greetings to the State Legislature from the country of Korea.

That evening, State Senator Kremer invited me to dinner at the Lincoln Hotel. In the dining room, I noticed a man intently reading his Bible as he ate. That's the kind of man I want to know. So I went up to him and asked him, "Are you a Christian?" He answered, "Yes, indeed. I am a pastor of the Seventh Day Adventist Church in Denver and I am here as a speaker for the Pastor's Conference. Where are you from?"

I told him a few things about myself. He was keenly interested and asked if I would explain the orphanage situation in Korea that evening at the pastor's conference. He said he would contact the chairman immediately. Before long, there was a telephone call from the conference chairman. We had a wonderful meeting and a good discussion afterwards.

This experience reminded me that the central issue is salvation through Christ. The Adventists emphasize seventh day worship, of course. But when I wake up I can't tell Monday from Tuesday. Really these are just names we give the days. When God created them we didn't have a language to record it. I believe the creation story that on the seventh day, God rested. But who knows what day that was? If they want to stay strictly by the time, Nebraska's Saturday is twenty-one hours behind the Korean Saturday. Speaking of time, I am so glad that we won't need watches in heaven. What a joy to be able to talk for ever!

Everywhere I went, people were especially interested in the matter of revival. As I testified about someone's stealing my church and the early morning prayer meetings for revival, many were convicted about their own churches. They realized that America needs revival as much as Korea does.

At one chapel service, after the meeting, the people decided together to have a prayer meeting for themselves every morning to pray for revival. They admitted that since they had both heating and seating they had no excuse. I am praying that the first daybreak service in the United States will start a revival in the whole country. Is it a dream?

§ "SAN DIEGO GOD" (July 1967)

I arrived in San Diego by Greyhound. I had some addresses in my pocket so I was not worried. But for two hours, I could not get one single answer on the telephone.

Then I remembered that a lady in Monterey had talked to me about her daughter and son-in-law who was in the ministry near San Diego. I checked through my letters and found their name. From the phone book, I was able to locate their number and establish contact. I stayed with Rev. and Mrs. Ruis for a few nights. They were missionaries to northern Mexico.

Through them the doors began to open. All the meetings were good, but one at the Armed Forces center really proved again God's power. As I testified, three Chinese Navy officers accepted Christ. After the meeting, we had a private discussion together and they really gave their lives to Him. Two weeks later they were baptized in the Scott Memorial Baptist Church. Again it showed the effectiveness of an Asian witnessing to an Asian. My slight knowledge of the Chinese language and customs helped a great deal.

Another Sunday evening I spoke at the College Avenue Baptist Church. Afterward the college group invited me to the beach. From 9:30 to 11:00 we talked together about the problems of youth and how Christ was the answer. One girl who looked like a hippie (she had long hair, a guitar and no shoes), stood up and said she wanted to accept Christ. She presented an honest testimony of how she was searching and knew Christ could help. Because of her witness, several teenagers followed and confessed Christ too.

§ **"LEARNING HOW TO DRIVE"** (September 1967)

I was really thrilled today when God provided a car for my travels. Because of the many meetings and busy schedule this was a real answer to prayer.

My driver was a young fellow who had led a rough life, and since he didn't have anything else to do, he agreed to be my chauffeur until he found a job.

He was not a Christian and so he grew tired of meetings, meetings, meetings. One afternoon he asked if he could be free instead of going with me to the meeting. Promising to be back by 9:00 when the church meeting would be over, he went to the beach at Oceanside, California. At 9:00 I returned to the car. But he hadn't shown up. I waited and waited and looked all around the beach. I called out for him, but there wasn't an answer. Two hours later he still was not anywhere around.

I had a meeting scheduled early the next morning in San Diego. I had to do something with the car before then, because I would be gone a number of days. After thinking about it, I decided to take the car off the street and park it in a church lot. I thought this would be a safe place while I was gone. I had driven a motorcycle in Korea, but had never touched the steering wheel of a car.

Slowly and carefully I backed into the street and headed for the parking lot. *This is fun,* I thought. My mind was one hundred percent attentive to the car and the road. After reaching the lot I practiced stopping, starting, turning. But turning was not easy. I held on to the wheel to turn it both back and forth.

Later I discovered that cars are not like motorcycles, but they correct themselves.

From the lot, I headed back down town for a little variety. By then all the traffic had gone. I found that driving along the streets was even easier than the parking lot, because the roads were straight. For thirty minutes, I practiced on the streets.

Meanwhile, I began thinking about my meeting in the morning. The suitcase in the trunk was full of literature and the meeting was scheduled for an early hour. Perhaps I could make it all the way by myself with the car! I ventured the forty miles on the freeway without a hitch. I made it!

As soon as I had some free time from the meetings, I went down to the local Motor Vehicle Department. I told the lady at the information desk that I needed a driver's license. She asked me if I had a license already. I said, "Yes," because I had a Korean motorcycle license. And so I filled out my application form and she gave me a long test paper with thirty-six questions.

I really had to wrestle with this examination. I hadn't studied the rule book and my limitations in English hindered me. I wasn't sure what I was doing, but after two long hours I was able to answer all of the questions except four. These I just didn't understand. So I took the paper and went to the window and explained my problem to the clerk. He said to me, "Where are you from?" I told him I was from Korea. He retorted: "Well, why don't you answer these questions then? You speak English better than many foreigners who take the test." I told him that I was sorry, but that the vocabulary in these four questions still had me confused. So he explained them to me and I checked the answers. When he corrected my test, I was happy that there were only three which I had missed!

Now came the driver's test. The man told me to get in line and wait my turn to be examined on the road. As I waited in line, I started talking about the exam to a young fellow in front of me. He told me that parallel parking would be a terrific problem. "Is that very difficult?" I asked. He was surprised: "Haven't you practiced yet?" I had to admit that I hadn't even heard about it until that moment. He suggested that I pull my car out of the line while the examiner was away and practice a bit.

I went to the place where they had two parking markers, and after backing up and going forward six or seven times I was finally in. But I couldn't get out. I looked back and didn't see anyone, so I started pulling away and knocked over a couple of the front poles in the process. I was discouraged and almost gave up. There was fighting inside. One half of my heart said that perhaps God wanted to save my life by not letting me pass. The other half said that I needed a license to do my job.

I looked around and saw a young lady execute a perfect parallel park. This made me angry. In Korea there are no lady drivers. Driving is a job for men, since most transportation is public. So I walked over to the test area to find the secret. I observed that the next five cars used almost the exact same method. They would pull up to the front of the marker, then back up until half the car was in the parking zone, and at that point they would begin to turn. And just as the car cleared the post, they would turn in the other direction. I was beginning to get the idea.

Taking a piece of chalk, I marked a line down the center of the back windows and side windows. When the tester went away again, I experimented in the parking space. This time I made it. Twice! Now I have a California driver's license.

§ **"PRESENTING WORLD CRISES TO YOUTH"** (February 1968)

By this time, my number of contacts had grown tremendously. The month of February found me in the State of Arizona, speaking in sixty-eight high school assemblies to over 27,000 public school students. The contacts with the schools were established easily because of a letter I received on February 2 from Mr. Herschel Hooper, director of secondary education, department of public instruction, State of Arizona:

"It is a pleasure to introduce to you this visitor from South Korea who has appeared before many high school and college departments and assemblies in California and Arizona. Reports from these addresses would indicate that he is a most fascinating speaker whose personal history and informative ideas create exceptional interest among our youth.

"Mr. Song is a high type Christian gentleman who feels impelled to express the gratitude of his people to the citizens of the United States. As more nations join the 'hate America group,' it is refreshing to learn of the lasting friendship of the people of South Korea."

My address usually centered on my life story which expressed thanks to America's mission program. I then went on to discuss Korean customs, history of war, present world problems, and my observations about the United States.

I found that most of the students listened attentively and respectfully. Most of them were sincere and wanted to know the truth. Only a small portion seemed to be negative and involved in wrong activities. Often I told them: "Most of you teenagers are the best teenagers in the world. And a few of you are the worst teenagers anywhere in the world."

The problem is that television and newspapers want to present the sensational, and so they seem to concentrate on the few evildoers. The problem is compounded by the fact that many parents are not communicating with their children. And then when something unusual happens, they immediately imagine the worst. Often they first think the bad things of young people and accuse them, before expecting the best. No wonder the kids rebel.

It always seems helpful in communicating with American teenagers to outline the four principles of living that we have in Korea. Eight hundred years under the influence of Confucian philosophy has formed this way of life in Korea.

First: Respect your parents. On special days (like Christmas, birthdays, New Year) almost all children in Korea bow to their parents before breakfast to show they have respect for them. Children are taught that all authority really belongs to the parents. Because of this principle, when a girl marries, she does not change her last name. My wife's name is Mrs. Kathy Lee. In America, my wife and I could not even use the same hotel room. This is a strange country!

Second: Respect your elders. Because we respect and obey elders we have at least six different names for people of different age and rank. All of them must be addressed properly. There are different words to use depending on the person to whom we are speaking.

In Korea, everyone wants to be older, not younger as in America. When a child is born, he is automatically one year old. And if he is born in December, even though it's only one month, when the new year begins he is two! Everyone in Korea is anxious to reach forty years of age. They even fib to hurry the years along. Why? Once you are over forty, everyone has to use polite terminology in addressing you.

Children do respect elders in Korea. Do you know why? From

the first grade, we Koreans read up and down. As we read we are saying, "Yes mom, yes teacher." And when we read the Bible we are saying yes to Jesus. But English is read from left to right. And as you're reading from side to side, your head is saying "No; no father, no teacher, no pastor." And the Bible? "I cannot believe this stuff, except perhaps John 3:16." And thus so many of the Western youngsters grow up with a negative attitude about life.

Third: Obey the king (government). We have grown up accepting the orders of the king. Whether right or wrong, we obey. Many have been killed by wicked rulers, but still the people accept this principle.

Fourth: Obey your husband. Shortly after I arrived in the United States, after a church meeting I rode home with a charming couple. They asked me, "If you don't mind, we want to stop at the market." Of course, it was no problem at all. The store where they stopped was a huge place. The husband jumped out from the car and rushed around to the other side to open the door for her. I was a little puzzled. I noticed she had a handbag in her left hand. But her right hand was free. I thought to myself: *she must have some problem with her hand.* I noticed, too, that he followed her to the market—something a little strange since in Korea the man goes first.

When they came out again, the wife wasn't carrying a thing and the husband had both his arms full with the two bags. He struggled over to the trunk to open it and place the bags inside. She stood there waiting for him. He opened the door for her again. I was sure she had a serious problem, a paralyzed side or something.

Today I understand this strange American custom. But I'm glad I was born in Korea. In Korea, the man goes with nothing. The wife follows on behind, with the baby on her back, grocery bags in her arms, and all the rest. He never looks back to see how she is doing.

But don't misunderstand. Certainly we as Christians must realize that men and women are equal under God. We simply must realize that in one or two days you cannot change a long tradition.

As I am talking with the teenagers, they usually ask me to give my impressions of the young people in the United States. I try to avoid this question by telling them I would rather be their friend than tell them exactly what I think. But they always insist that I go ahead and say what I please.

I think that seventy percent of the youth of America are the best young people, full of compassion and creative minds. But on the other hand, about fifteen percent of the youth of America seem to rebel. Anywhere in the world you can find a small percentage of rebellious young people.

I can understand why the young people in Asia rebel, due to the lack of education and material wealth. But I find it hard to understand why American youth rebel, with so many opportunities and materials. They seem to have all that they could ever want.

I see teenagers' hang-ups in terms of the four S's—at least that makes it easy to remember.

1. Screen. So many teenagers sit in front of the TV and movie screen, just wasting time instead of studying. TV is all right, but time could be better spent doing constructive things. I don't mean you shouldn't watch the screen—Saturday for example. But TV shouldn't become a god for your life.

I observed people coming out of a theater one day and noticed that over half were under twelve years of age. Why? Because it's cheaper than babysitting. When Mom and Dad are gone in the afternoon, they sometimes find it easier to send their kids to the theater instead of taking care of them themselves. Children are well entertained there, they say, and young ones do not cost anything. But the theater is not a nursery. It is not designed to give us good educational food.

2. Speed. The freeways, the fast cars, and preoccupation with living a fast life leaves no time for just good hard thinking about life itself! The remarkable thing about America is all the cars, and especially all the lady drivers.

Shortly after arriving here I had the opportunity to ride with a sixty-seven-year-old lady who promised to take me down a California freeway to another town. As she raced along at seventy miles per hour, I was scared and finally mustered the courage to ask her to slow down. She asked, "Are you kidding me?" So I told her I wasn't, but was really scared. "My problem is, I can't trust lady drivers." She reassured me that all would be all right, and it was. We made it.

There are many, many freeways to rush here and there. No time is left for family and for meditation. Teenagers' lives are terribly speedy too. The competition for dates with the right girls and long conversations on the phone, keeping up with the latest sports—all of this makes time for studying quite limited.

The Christian life is not one of speed, it is one of direction. In Los Angeles, it was my experience that once we had lost our direction, it made no difference whether we were going seventy miles an hour or not. Where we are going is important. The Christian needs time to make sure of his direction.

3. Self. All around the world teenagers are selfish, putting themselves above every other person. But affluence complicates the problem even more. When there is great poverty, everyone depends much on others. As young people we need the help our parents can give, for example. But in America it seems the youth grow up on their own, with all the money and ability to run their own lives. This tends to make them even more selfish. Perhaps a reminder is important here: We must always give first place to God, second place to others, and last place to ourselves.

4. Sex. Let's not get into details about it, but teenagers all over this country are obsessed with sex. One Saturday night in California I was the speaker at a Youth for Christ rally, so I arrived about twenty minutes before the meeting started. In the audience I saw a 16-year-old girl with a baby on her lap. So I asked her: "How much money do you earn for baby sitting?" She replied: "Sir, this is my baby." I was surprised and wanted to know more.

I asked where her husband was. She pointed to the young boy next to her and called him "Ricky." I asked him whether he was attending high school. This started him on a long story of how he had quit and presently was holding down several jobs in order to pay all the family expenses. I felt terribly sorry for him. Obviously he was not satisfied and he was facing the Viet Nam draft. Already at his age he was facing insurmountable obstacles with his house, car, furniture, and all the rest.

I have often wondered why there are so many divorces in the United States. Could early marriages like these be one reason? In Korea, such marriages are not permitted since the parents of both bride and groom have to approve. The war has also complicated the situation. The girl's parents especially do not want early marriage before the fellow goes off to war. They are concerned about their daughters becoming widows.

On many occasions I am asked about the hippies. My immediate response is that in Korea boys and girls dress in the same kind of uniforms and all the girls wear the same hair styles and all the fellows' hair is cut in the same way. So we don't have any hippies in Korea.

And then they ask, "But what about American hippies?" I tell them plainly that I don't like them. "Why not?" "Because it looks dirty to me," I responded. But they persist: "What do you think of the movement, not just of the people involved?"

My rejoinder this time is a clear example from language. The senior is Tom, his junior is Tommy. Sam and Sammy, Ben and Benny have that difference too. I think hippy is from the senior word, hypocrisy—and I don't care for hypocrisy.

When they remind me that something must be lacking in society today and the hippies are trying to challenge the adults to do something creative about it, I have to agree. But isn't it better, when you see something wrong, to be the new leader of tomorrow rather than follow the way of hypocrisy?

"Well," the president of a student body asked, "what would you do about it if you were governor?"

My answer is emphatic: "If it were possible to become a governor in the United States, I would ship out all the hippies to the Viet Nam jungles for the twelve-month period that other young men from America must serve. I think then they would appreciate the good they have in the United States."

Young people are always asking me about the present world situation. My usual explanation is that I don't worry so much about the world situation, as about the internal, national situation in the United States.

I am confident that Chinese Communists could not invade South Korea. But I do see them making an invasion inside the United States, through race riots, youth dope addictions, immoral propaganda in society, divisions in the homes, political fighting and any other method which breaks down the unity and strength of a nation.

§ "DALE EVANS: MOTHER TO THE LEAST" (February 1968)

I saw Dale Evans and Roy Rogers on the movie screen in Korea, and heard much about their generous support of Korean orphans. Never did I dream that I would see them personally or be able to stay in their home. In fact, I have now received a key so that I can stay there whenever I am in that part of California.

While visiting them, I discovered how busy Dale was in her witnessing for the Lord. There are always numerous speaking engagements. Right now she is busy writing her ninth book. They are supposed to be retired from an active work life, yet there is more to do now than ever.

Their concern for Korean orphans makes me feel right at home. You probably remember the story of their daughter Debbie. She was an adopted Korean girl who was killed at the age of 12 in 1964 when a church bus crashed. It was a mission tour bus, on the way to Mexico. Debbie is only one of several children they have adopted into their home.

While staying with them, I engaged in some conversation with the dear lady who helped take care of Debbie, Mrs. Ruth Miner. I asked her how many books Dale had written. She told me about some of them. She further explained that the royalties for many of her books went to charities. Her best seller was written about the death of their retarded child, Robin. Dale titled it *Angel Unawares* to tell the story of the impact this little girl made in their home.

The Rogers have become tremendously famous and have won numerous awards over the years. Dale was once named "Mother of the Year." Roy is still known today as the "King of Cowboys." I wondered why they lived in this modest home in the desert countryside. I asked Mrs. Miner about it and she replied: "Their careers do not matter anymore as they used to. They are always involved in other activities and with people rather than themselves."

One evening we shared until midnight what the Lord was doing. One of Dale's comments really touched my heart: "I had been searching for years for fame and honor. I wanted to be the best movie actress possible and have all the material things the world could give. Yet I could find no answer. But, Ben, when I met Jesus, I found living water just like the woman at the well in Sychar." Once again I was shown how powerful the Spirit and the Word of God really are to change the heart of anyone—even those who are rich and famous.

§ **"SUITCASE SERMON"** (February 1968)

In my travels, many people sign a pledge that they will pray for my ministry. These interested people ask me to write them often and explain how the Lord is using me. But the list of addresses grew so long after a while, that I couldn't write them individually anymore. Miraculously the Lord provided two men in Ventura, California, to help print a monthly letter. Tonight I am sitting down to write my letter, my suitcase sermon, to my many friends:

"Greetings from the Grand Canyon State, latest stop of your Suitcase Missionary.

"Praise His wonderful Name—Jesus Christ our Lord—for the many openings in Arizona and in California. I need your prayers especially for the school meetings that the students might hear the message and open their hearts to Christ and be saved. I also need your continued prayers for my many thousands of miles of driving across the country.

"Even as I write this letter, the world situation is tense due to the aggressive action of the North Korean Communists. Is it possible that God will again open the doors of North Korea? In the past, North Korea was a stronghold of Christianity. But believers there have suffered for twenty years now under the terrible persecutions of the Communists. I have an uncle and cousins in North Korea but I do not know whether or not they are Christians. We have many pastors living in South Korea who had to flee from North Korea for their lives. They have lived alone without any word from their families for all these many years.

"We do not know what will take place, but we know that *God is sovereign* and He can do the impossible through these circumstances. Do you realize that North Korea holds the key to one of the main doors into Red China? Can it be that God will give China another chance to hear the Gospel?

"For the most part, Asian countries have never had mass evangelistic campaigns where thousands could hear the Gospel at once. The Chinese Communists have destroyed all the false religions and philosophies through their brain-washing techniques. The masses of China are empty and God may turn an apparent victory for Satan into a victory for Jesus Christ. The Bible says that this Gospel must be preached to all nations and then the end shall come.

"As I write to you this evening, my heart cries out for many lost souls throughout Asia, especially those under Communist domination. We do not know how much longer we can preach the Gospel to the lost. We must seize every opportunity in the future. We must be ready to send native evangelists into these countries as the doors open—using mass evangelism and literature.

"America and the world today are so concerned about another world war. And we should be. I know personally how terrible war is. But not many are concerned about the immoral propaganda that is flooding society through our television sets, or about the widespread and rapidly increasing youth dope addiction—or about the racial strife and riots which are occurring in this country.

"The battle in these last days is not physical or military only, but underlying all of the turmoil is the spiritual warfare between the forces of God and Satan. And the battleground is in the minds and hearts of men! Are we winning or losing this battle? We are not winning it, and neither are we losing it. *We are simply forfeiting it!*

"How is the battle being forfeited? Dear friend, the Great Commission commands us: 'Go ye into all the world and preach the gospel to every creature!' We are having our last chance now to reach our generation. What are we waiting for? God has been calling us to total commitment ever since the day we were saved. He wants *total commitment* from us *today!*

"You can serve Him full time in this battle. I realize that not everyone can go to Asia as a missionary, but you can help support those who are on the field, and help train young people to serve full time as missionaries in the harvest field of Asia. How? You could sacrifice one meal a week and be able to send $5.00 each month for this work. Four friends giving $5.00 each per month can pay the cost of training a Korean national worker. And four giving $10.00 per month can support one of these workers on a full-time basis.

"I have a great desire to return to my homeland and to rejoin my family and co-workers in the ministry. But the Lord has opened doors for me to spend another few months in the United States, and at this writing I am in Phoenix and plan to go on to New Mexico, Texas, Oklahoma, and into the states of the Midwest before returning to Korea. There is so little time left and yet there are so many places where I must preach the Gospel. I know you are praying for me and that we are laborers together with God in this great work.

"Won't you join with me in prayer for these goals:

"1. *Increase the number of native Asian missionaries.* Do you know that some countries are not open for Western missionaries (Hungary, India, Cambodia, Pakistan, etc.), but are still open for Oriental and native workers? Also, concerning cost, we could send out twelve native missionaries for one foreign missionary, due to living expenses and time for taking three years of language study. This is important and effective because time is short. Native evangelists can communicate more easily than foreigners in Asia. Doesn't the Bible say, 'The harvest is ready and there are few laborers'?

"2. *All Asia evangelistic crusades.* In Korea, Japan, Viet Nam, and Indonesia, if the Lord is willing, we are going to have major city-wide crusades and train soul-winning workers. The daytime will be spent in lay training institutes and the evenings set aside for crusades.

"3. *Asian Ambassadors for Christ team in the U. S. A.* Of course, I don't forget my benefactor, the United States. I can see a great need for ministering to youth here. The Asian team will be traveling in the high schools and colleges of the United States with their country's customs, history, music and personal testimonies for Christ. We do this with thanksgiving that America made it possible to evangelize Asia. After the team covers cities from state to state, we will have a Youth Crusade.

"Let me close my suitcase now, but it's really difficult because this suitcase has so much to say. As I was driving to the schools in my station wagon, students were amused and questioned me about the bumper sticker on my car which reads: 'Our God is Alive . . . Sorry About Yours.' While talking with the young people I offer them a sticker for their cars as a challenge to their friends. My suitcase says that there are only twelve left.

"How do I get in? I cannot answer, except to say: 'He set before me an open door, and no man can shut it.' This is the power of God. Continue to pray for open doors.

"Do I give an invitation? Of course. One approach is to ask them if they respect George Washington, Abraham Lincoln, and then how about Jesus Christ. I tell them I am not talking about religion, but I am talking about one Person who has done greater things than these wonderful men. I ask them if they want to know more details of Korean history, my story and salvation through Jesus Christ, I will give them my life-story booklet and talk to them after the meeting. Dozens always come forward to inquire personally, sixty-eight at one school and thirty at another. The luncheon time is the most valuable of all for personal contact. Yesterday I mailed 126 follow-up materials to interested students. For this I praise God.

"My hair has not been growing fast enough to keep my private barbers in business.

"My suitcase tells me to keep enough material for the next sermon. No, I have to tell about church meetings too. Please, a little more. I will be on TV which is a great opportunity.

"Miracle after miracle — only half told — because of your prayers. Can't wait to share what God will do tomorrow.

"Let us (my suitcase too) say goodnight; it is past twelve midnight. With love in our soon coming Lord.

"Ben Song, under Calvary's bondage, with suitcase on the road."

§ "SCHEDULING SCHOOL MEETINGS" (May 1968)

I don't have any personnel for scheduling my school meetings. I just drop by different schools in my travels. For example, if I'm traveling up Highway 101 in California, I stop approximately every hour and go to the nearest school and present my credentials to the principal. I then make arrangements for one month later. As I come down Highway 99 I repeat the same procedure. Consequently, I'm booked solid for a month or two ahead of time.

The following is one of the many letters received from principals which is good recommendation for other schools:

"To Whom It May Concern:

Just by chance, Mr. Ben Song came to my office on April 30 and offered his services as a speaker before our students. He wanted to do this in appreciation for having received his education through a gift of $10.00 per month made to him, a Korean orphan, by an American donor.

"I have been associated with young men and women in public schools for almost forty years and I can say without hesitation that I have never seen another person captivate his audience as Mr. Song has done today. He talked in three separate assemblies in our gymnasium, to the sophomores, juniors and the seniors. The seniors gave Mr. Song a standing ovation at the close of his talk which is the first time in the history of our school that this has taken place.

"To anyone who wishes an inspired, down-to-earth speaker, I would unhesitatingly recommend Mr. Song. Our senior class has invited him back to speak to them in their government classes, such is their admiration for his ability as a speaker."

Keith Gunn, Principal
Victor Valley Senior High School
Victorville, California 92392

The following is another example of wonderful reception by students:

"Mr. Song was one of the most interesting and unusual speakers I've heard. This man truly has a story to tell. He'd been through a lot of hardship and pain in his life. He is truly grateful for every day he is alive after seeing his family and others executed. His points on how the English language is very confusing is very true also. His points on the way Americans are always in a hurry are so true. The Californians are more so than the people back East. I wish more of us would be grateful that we have many things and luxuries as we have. I would enjoy having him back."

Sandy Smith

". . . He really expressed the point of Christianity. I began to think how lucky we are to have churches to attend and we can attend whichever one we want. In conclusion he made me feel not only honored to be an American but also to be a Christian."

Judy Anderson

"I accepted Christ when you spoke at our school. I appreciate your life story booklet and salvation letter. They really helped me a lot. But I find it difficult to coincide my Christianity with my school activities."

Jacqueline

The wonderful things that are happening here in the United States are almost unbelievable. In the past I've taken combined classes and assemblies in the high schools. Now I will be taking assemblies only, because it is an opportunity to reach more youth at one time. For example, I have spoken to 24,000 students in January and 22,300 in February this year. *In this way I am able to reach tomorrow's leaders where they are today.* I will also be continuing to present challenges to Christians in the churches.

Today I received a letter from Mrs. A. McLeich which brought great encouragement to me. Let me share some of her letter with you:

"What a 'mountaintop experience' actually seeing for myself the way you are able to reach high school youth! To stand with them as they gave you their standing ovation at Monclaire High, I could but prayerfully, silently say, 'Thank You God, for sending Ben Song to us.'

"Another mother shared this experience with me. Her son attends another school in our district and her immediate desire was that her boy and all youth could have the privilege of hearing your 'Thank You.' I could assure her that you were reaching the youth in the five high schools of the Chaffey School District and that over ten thousand youth of our local areas were scheduled to hear you.

"Ben, if only all parents could experience, as did the two of us, the eagerness of those youth, and their hunger for something 'positive'—through straight talk and humor—to which they could personally relate. We saw you successfully communicate, where we as parents cannot. They automatically 'tune us out' where they 'tuned you in.' They were listening and were identifying with you the entire hour!

"As the wife of the associate superintendent of Chaffey High School District, as a mother of twin sons (age sixteen), and as a former teacher and guidance director for high school, I am writing you with deep appreciation for what you are doing through His help. Bless you."

Mrs. A. McLeich, Ontario, California

§ **"PRAY FOR ME"** (July 1968)

I return to my country with an immeasurable burden on my heart.

God has answered prayer in unusual ways for our world-wide ministry. Never has the hunger for Jesus Christ been greater. Our outreach to the rag pickers in the slums, the outcast blind, the criminals in prison, the thousands of forgotten in the countryside, the millions across Asia, the youth and unsaved in America —God has increased these opportunities a hundredfold.

Pray for my family, our staff, for myself. I'm praying for you and thank God for your wonderful country.

Ben becomes a suitcase
missionary to U. S.

Opportunities came
to speak just everywhere

High school
ministry develops.

Happy reunion after long 20 months' separation.

Appendix

SHARING FROM MY HEART TO YOURS

§ "THROUGH THE LENS OF THE CROSS"

I have been much amazed at all the denominations in America (someone told me, 376). In Korea this isn't true—just the major denominations are represented. After much observation and discussion, I have concluded that these many churches can be summarized into four different types. And these four types form the symbol of the cross.

One group is interested in emphasizing the truth, the Word of God. The vertical relationship of man to God is the most crucial to them and this is strongly proclaimed from the pulpit. Often these churches are called fundamental. They promote the letter of the law when it comes to Christian living.

Another group is also interested basically in the vertical relationship and these we might call the formalistic churches. Worship with beauty and elegance is very important to them. They want to honor and glorify Him in a dignified way.

The horizontal piece on the cross has always symbolized the relationship of man to man. A third group might be placed at one end of the piece and called "holiness." Sanctification by the power of the Holy Spirit is extremely significant to them. They put a healthy concentration on the need of men to mature spiritually and to attain as much perfection as possible.

The fourth group of churches is found at the other end of the horizontal piece. These are the liberal churches. They are socially concerned, they have the compassion to reach out to fellow men. Love is always mentioned as the key way of life. Ethics are stressed and people are encouraged to do good.

Each one of the groups has a weakness. Fundamentalism often concentrates too much on the letters of the law, and legalism will not save souls. Formalism is often external, without the heart being right with God. Ritualism is powerless to redeem. To stress holiness out of proportion is not to be honest with our sin; and surely emotionalism itself will not bring salvation. Socialism without Christ is a subtle way of presenting all kinds of good answers, without really proclaiming the only answer, Christ Himself. Socialism cannot save souls.

All who believe in salvation through Christ have come in a slightly different way. These together make up the body of Christ and we must learn an appreciation of this oneness in Him. A vertical piece of wood does not make a cross. A horizontal piece does not make a cross. Both are important. The Bible explains both God-man relationships and man-man relationships. God is a God both of justice and love. There is always the eternal and today at the same moment.

The Bible tells us to be the salt of the earth. Salt is composed of two deadly poisons: sodium and chloride. If you take a spoon of pure sodium, you will die immediately. But when the two are combined, they form salt which is harmless, in fact one of the most necessary items in the world. Christianity is composed of two deadly poisons: theology and ethics, faith and practice. Take theology by itself, and the Christian would be killed. Take ethics by itself, with all the do-goodism possible and we would be killed. "Faith without works is dead." Yet we are "saved by faith, not of works lest any man should boast."

Many Christians argue about election and "whosoever will." I don't have any problem. Outside the gate of heaven is written the words for all to see and believe: "Whosoever will may come." This is for every unbeliever. But on the inside of the gate of heaven is written: "Chosen from the foundation of the world." This truth is God's promise for believers.

Let us not argue too much about the differences. If anyone believes in salvation through Christ and believes in Christ as personal Saviour we must be open to Him and cooperate where possible. God would want us to be interested in the ninety-five percent for His Kingdom.

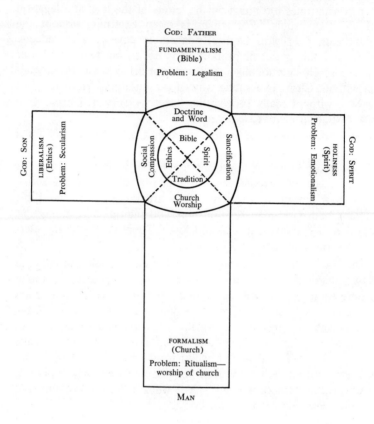

The cross teaches us:

Vertically	*Horizontally*
1. God and man relationship	1. Man and men fellowship
2. Believing Jesus Christ	2. Accepting Jesus Christ
3. Eternal God	3. Today God
4. Westernism, No!	4. Orientalism, No!
5. Knowing God	5. Trusting God
6. Sound theology	6. Total commitment
7. Worship God	7. Love others
8. Personal experience	8. Personal expression

§ "THREE TEMPTATIONS"

In the fourth chapter of Matthew we find Jesus led into the wilderness to be tempted by Satan. Jesus fasted forty days and nights, and became very hungry. At this point the tempter said to Jesus: "If you are the Son of God, command these stones to become loaves of bread." Yes, surely Jesus was hungry. He must have wanted to make bread from these stones. But He answered, "Man shall not live by bread alone, but by every word that proceeds out of the mouth of God."

There are two principles by which man can live. First: What he wants to do according to his own wishes. Second: What he must do according to the Bible. What he wants to do is man's will. What man has to do is God's will.

Certainly we need bread and many material things. But man shall not live by bread alone. First—God; second—others; and third—ourselves. Jesus was tempted to make bread but He had to follow God's will. How about us? Are we busy making bread or following God's Word?

Satan said: "If you are the Son of God." How many so-called Christian churches today express this same doubt? *If* you are the Son of God. He *was* the Son of God. He *is* the Son of God, yesterday, today, and forever. Jesus is always the same. Don't worry about the God-is-dead business. My God is the living God!

The second temptation began when Satan took Jesus to the top of the temple and said, "If you are the Son of God, cast yourself down." Here we have the same doubts expressed. *If* you are. And the top of the temple is very dangerous! It's easy to fall, so be careful. Big names and self-importance, even in church, have their dangers. Our human lives tend to be centered on ourselves. Man likes to show himself.

Then Satan said: "Cast yourself down." The Christian life is not only miracles. We must enter into the temple, kneel down, confess our sins, stand by grace, walk by faith, and finally ascend by the power of Jesus' coming.

Notice too that Satan used the Scriptures from the Psalms, but he misquoted them. Some parts were left out, some changed, and some added. But God's Word is not to be changed. We cannot leave out even a comma. We must believe the whole Bible.

Many denominations in existence today have depended upon

parts of Scripture, adding some, changing others to fit their own doctrines. Let us not misquote Scripture to fit our own ideas. We must accept the whole Bible. God's Word has the power, so Jesus overcame these difficult temptations. Praise God. Thank God for this Bible. The Bible tells us that Jesus loves us, He died for us, and we are one body in Him. Let's be one family.

The third temptation occurred when Satan took Jesus up into a high mountain and showed Him all the kingdoms of the world and the glory of them. And Satan said: "All these things will I give you if you will fall down and worship me." In this world there are many kingdoms: wealth, wisdom, prominence, sports, and enjoyment. This world is built of small kingdoms. But this world is not our home. We are strangers here. Our home is in heaven.

Satan took Jesus to the highest mountain in the world which was an important place. The world really looked attractive from there. And Satan said: "Fall down and worship me and I will give you all." This would have been easy. So Satan is using an easy religion in these days. Some doctrines even tell us to relax. "Just fall down," he says.

But Jesus had to go to another mountain. Then He said: "Pick up your cross and follow Me." Certainly Christianity is not a religion. It is walking with Jesus. I can't do this by myself. Praise God, we can do everything with Jesus. In this world there are two mountains: the glory-of-the-world mountain and Calvary mountain. Are we going to the right mountain? Even those who sometimes want to carry the cross (some social workers and businessmen, for example) end up with the cross carrying them.

Do you love your neighbors? Do you love the least of these my brethren? Jesus promised us: "If you give a cup of cold water to drink to one of the little ones, you shall not lose your reward in heaven." Christianity is a willing journey to Calvary's mountain.

§ "REVIVAL FLAMES THROUGH TRIAL"

It was the year 1968 on the Western calendar and the Korean calendar showed 4301—a rather amazing fact! Korea traces her history across 4300 years and yet what the American people know about Korea they have learned in only the last twenty years.

Why only the last twenty years? It was suddenly on a June

morning of 1950 that Korea exploded literally into significance. The event focused world-wide attention and it took the lives of over 30,000 American fighting men to etch the map of Korea in blood on the heart of every American family. And so it has been down through the centuries that all of the decisive changes in Korea's national history have come to the accompaniment of tramping feet and battle music.

Go back to the thirteenth century and you find that the Mongolian barbarians far to the north attempted an invasion of the island empire of Japan and used the little peninsula of Korea as a natural pathway and left it a shambles.

In 1594 the Japanese attempted an invasion of China and once again used the peninsula of Korea as a pathway to that great nation in the northwest. Korea was again left in devastation. Only fifty years later the Manchus directly to the north of Korea, seeing her weakened condition, came down to take advantage of it. Korea was destroyed once more.

In the years 1904 and 1905 came the Russo-Japanese war. Although Korea was not an active participant in this warfare, yet it was caught up in a very real way in the military struggle. It was at this time the Japanese made a landing on the north coast of Korea in a little harbor called Inchon. Many years later General MacArthur was to do the same. There the Japanese gained a foothold in Korea that they never relinquished until 1945.

And then, of course, in 1950 came the Communist aggression across the 38th parallel. During this time some of the worst atrocities we have ever heard of in the course of history were committed.

I repeat, the most decisive changes in Korea's national history have come to the accompaniment of battle music. But no less than the nation, the church in Korea has seen her most decisive moment during the nation's darkest hour. Christian missions began in Korea in the year 1885 with the arrival of two pioneer missionaries.

During the two subsequent decades it was very difficult to preach the Gospel openly. Korea, for centuries, had been known as a hermit kingdom. It preferred to remain as a recluse among the nations of the world, enclosing her mountains around herself. The people wanted to ward off any infiltration of Western ideas. They wanted to retain their "pure blood" and all their "traditional culture." Confucianism did not tolerate any influence of the Christian religion.

It is said that for a great period of time, Koreans burned strips all along their coast line so that their coast would seem barren and devoid of life to passing ships. So the Gospel had to be brought in rather subtle ways.

It was during the war of 1904-1905 that revival really began. Out of the struggle and worry and troubles, Christianity emerged. It was only a few years after Christian missionaries had come, so the number of converts was small. This little group began praying earnestly for the country. They asked God to send a revival.

For several months these prayer meetings continued. But nothing seemed to happen. The only thing that grew was the intensity of the Japanese occupation. It was then that they began realizing their focus was wrong. They discovered that instead of praying for a revival in the country, God should send it into their own hearts.

This was the key. The revival began to come. The word spread and Christians prayed more earnestly that God would move. The intensity of the prayers grew and revival flames spread. Perhaps, historically speaking, the church began in 1885. But spiritually speaking the church was not born until the revival. It began in 1904 and by 1906-1907 a climax had been reached. Because of the occupation, the growth of the movement caused oppression. To avoid harassment, Christians began meeting for prayer early in the morning when the policemen and troops did not seem to bother. The next three years also saw the revival grow in power. In the peak year, more than 50,000 converts were added to the Korean church!

This is still remembered in history as the great era of revival in Korea. In 1910, as a result of this revival, three missionaries were sent to China from Korea. They served there until the Red Chinese took over control.

After the South-North Korean war, a great number of converts were added to the church. Before the war, the population was only .08 percent Christian. Now it is over 7 percent. Revival does not come from the outside, but from total dedication from within. Christianity has always repeated its history: A few dedicated men under oppression, starting with the apostles, who have no other choice but to depend one hundred percent on God.

This century is the most needy ever for revival. This atomic and technological age has made everyone sense an emptiness in their hearts. The most dangerous tendency in this century is a Christianity without Christ, religion without salvation, a way of life without love.

I believe we have the same power now as they had in the first century when an ignorant fisherman like Peter was touched and 3,000 souls were converted with one sermon. It is a sad fact, but true, that when someone is really happy today and really rejoicing, we tend to think he is not spiritual enough. In the face of present crises, often the churches are only giving discouragement rather than showing the joy of the Christian faith.

I was interested to observe recently a couple's conversation. The wife mentioned that the neighbors had a new TV set so they needed one too. She listed a whole series of things that they should be getting in order to have conveniences like the others in the block. Finally her husband said: "Honey, there's only one thing that we don't have." She was quite surprised and insisted that there were many things. His answer was a classic: "The only thing we don't have is money." It reminded me immediately of many comments we hear in the church today. Some insist we need to be better Christians, need more opportunities for service, need more cooperation and sympathy from others. To all of these the answer is simple: "We need the power of the Holy Spirit. This is the problem." If we are filled with the Holy Spirit moment by moment, already revival has begun in ourselves and this fire goes out to others.

Let me conclude with the secret of being filled with the Holy Spirit:

1. We must be drawn together often. The Bible commands us "not to depart from Jerusalem, but wait for the promise of the Father" (Acts 1:4). Logs have to be gathered into a pile to make a good fire. When they're all separate they do not burn well at all. So we must take seriously times of fellowship and prayer with other Christians.

2. We must not just repent, but really repent sincerely. Repentance is not just for one time, but every day. We must wash our faces every day, and the same thing is true for our Christian life.

3. We must earnestly learn to call upon God. "Call unto me, and I will answer thee and shew thee great and mighty things,

which thou knowest not" (Jeremiah 33:3). Prayer is the breath of the Christian life. We can't stop breathing, so as Christians we may not stop praying. All of our thinking and concern must be done in prayer.

4. Discuss the Word of God. At all times, we must be receiving our food from the Scriptures. Luke 22 says they were discussing the Word of God and then the power of the Holy Spirit came.

5. Patient and humble waiting for Him. All things happen for the glory of God and our good, so we must wait for His will. Many people are so anxious to have a supernatural feeling from God. Our trying will be of no value. It is all God's work.

These five secrets will give us a life of joy rather than fear. Through these steps revival can come even in a wicked, desert-like area. Remember the story of Jonah and how revival came to the city of Nineveh, capital of a pagan country.

§ "TWO MISSION MOVEMENTS"

Often on the radio and at political science assemblies in colleges, I am asked for my ideas on the Viet Nam war. Everyone wants to know, it seems. Many people are very close to each event in the war, discuss it often, study it deeply. Yet I wonder sometimes if they see it as it is in a fundamental sense—as a spiritual conflict.

My opinion about the war has to be explained in two different ways: political and spiritual. Politically speaking, I cannot see any military victory in Viet Nam. The biggest headache is the fact that we do not really know who the enemy is. But really, this war is not military to military, it is basically economy to economy. As a Korean, I cannot permit Communism to survive. It should not be allowed to exist anywhere on the earth. Every kind of military action should be taken to rid the world of its horrible manifestations. For this reason, the Republic of Korea is willing to send over 50,000 soldiers to assist in Viet Nam. This is from a country half the size of Utah.

Spiritually speaking, there are two kinds of missionary movements in the world today. Communism is a missionary movement that is extremely effective for youth, and poor, primitive countries. Why? Because Communism has a message which promises utopia by means of social power. It looks tremendously attractive. Communism tries to captivate the minds and wills of people from the youngest on up. The Christian missionary movement endeavors to win the people over to the glorious liberty of the living, risen Saviour.

In Korea, before the war, many Koreans were closed to the Gospel. During the war, satanic powers seemed to be unleashed. The steadfast testimony of many Christians encouraged the hearts of thousands. Besides this, the attention of many free countries was drawn to Korea because of the war. Countless missionaries of the cross were drawn there to win souls. The generous gifts of clothing, medicine, building materials, and literature (printed missionaries) touched the hardened hearts. This has resulted in over one and a half million Christians in Korea today. And we do not have even one party which is Communistic in South Korea. This has proved to me that Christianity is the most powerful threat to Communism today.

Do you realize that it takes a half million dollars to kill one Viet Cong in Viet Nam? But it costs an average of fifty cents to win an Asian soul to Christ. Winning people to Christ also makes them members of one family in Him. For one day's cost of the war, thousands of missionaries, advisors, professional nurses and doctors could start tremendous evangelism all over Viet Nam and Asia too. The Asians must be won to Christ before our Lord's return. I strongly believe Christ is the only answer—even for the world's war problems in this time of crisis and fear.

The sad fact is that this spiritual war is not limited to Korea or Viet Nam, but it's in the United States as well. Some years ago, a famous magazine reported on Communist movements outside of Communistic countries. 800,000 members of the Communist party were reported outside the Iron Curtain, with 86,000 of these in the United States itself.

It is to our shame that Communism seems more dedicated to Karl Marx than Christians are to Christ. Let us not forget, World War Three is on already.

§ "AMERICA IS SLEEPING"

Not only do we find riots, dope addiction and immoral propaganda on our college and university campuses, but also some of our young people are being trained in guerrilla warfare in order to destroy authority. Would you believe that the University of California at Santa Barbara has classes in guerrilla warfare three times a week?

There was a headline in the *Los Angeles Times* not long ago— "Disruptions Fail to Close Schools." Two days later, the headlines were "Schools Cry for Help." Even as I write you this evening, my heart cries out for the many who are caught up in all of these world-wide unrests. Souls are dying. Youth is being destroyed.

Here is a quotation from just one of the many pieces of unfavorable literature being distributed on the UCSB campus: "The Declaration of Independence clearly establishes that it is not only right, but indeed it is the duty of a citizen to overthrow the government of his country if it is no longer capable of responding to the needs of the people. Guerrilla warfare is the modern method of overthrowing governments. The purpose of this class is not to enlighten people into a revolutionary consciousness or to argue that our present government is incapable of responding to the people; it is the purpose of this class to give the people who are already convinced that this government needs to be overthrown, a method for overthrowing it. Politics will not be discussed in this class, although political awareness is absolutely necessary in any guerrilla movement, since only methods themselves will be discussed and practiced."

On the other side of the same paper are many questions. I will quote just two: "What are a few looted buildings compared to millions of looted lives?" "How can you build new buildings before you burn the old ones down?"

I have been asked many times for my comments about these conditions on the campuses. Through my experiences under the Communist occupation and their spying activities, I know that your enemies are not these students. It is Communism. These students do not know where they are going, with whom and for what.

America is sleeping. She has been sleeping far too long already. Through the "Voice of Freedom" in Korea, we were told that an estimated seven percent of students of college age in the United States are either involved in or agree with the demonstrations and revolutionary ideas. They further estimated that it will be over fifteen percent in 1972.

When the Communists overthrew the government of Russia they represented only about five percent of the total population. The overthrow of the mainland of China was accomplished by less than two percent of the people. Communism came to power in North Korea through the violence of a relatively small percentage of its citizens. The revolutionists were ruthless and murdered their own relatives and thousands of Christians.

The Communists believe that they will be able to overthrow the American government when they reach this goal of fifteen percent by 1972. I am amazed to find that most Americans are not concerned about the fact that Communism and revolutionary ideas have seized the minds of so many of the high school and college students.

Last summer, Communists held their first "World-Wide Communist Congress." At the meeting, Communists openly boasted that Communism is sweeping all over the world. It is winning World War III without firing a shot, or losing a single soldier.

We must not sit idly by. Let us warn and awaken the youth of America before it is too late. We have the positive answer— Jesus Christ. Evil influence is more powerful than Christian influence because of our human nature. But with Christ we receive eternal victory by faith. *We* cannot win against the old devil, but Christ has already won the victory through the cross and the empty tomb.

Many Americans, especially the young, are brainwashed through the various communication mediums. Some are blinded, and these are often idolized as the smart ones!

But not all are brainwashed. The following letter is indicative of the many letters from teachers who appreciate our efforts to awaken the teenagers to the dangers of Communism:

"In my fourteen years at Carpinteria High School as a teacher and administrator I don't ever recall a speaker who received such an enthusiastic ovation as you did. This in itself is a fine tribute and commentary to you and attests to your effectiveness and to the appreciation of the students.

"The teenagers of America, as you indicated in your speech, are looking for direction. I feel you answered many of their questions and helped to dispel some of their concerns about the future."

Sincerely,
Martin Koobation

The Student Body Council of Oxnard High School held an emergency meeting right after I spoke at the assembly. The president of the Student Council presented me with a $50.00 check and said, "This is given to help all American students hear your message." This experience was repeated in Montclair High also.

§ "GO SIGNAL!"

The Bible was written by the most sensitive and spiritual prophets of the time. Samuel was sensitive to David's role in the history of Israel. Ezra and Nehemiah understood the trends of history toward the end of the captivity under Nebuchadnezzar in Babylon. These men cried with tears and prayed to God for revival in the whole country.

According to Nehemiah 2:11, 12, the walls of Jerusalem had fallen, the gates were burned out and the people had scattered across the earth. There are many similarities to the situation today. The authority of Christianity has fallen down and its influence dissipated. Even without a country and under the judgment of God, there was adultery, hatred, injustice among the people. Today it seems exactly the same. Wickedness is rampant today as well.

Praise the Lord for Ezra and Nehemiah. They realized and sensed God's calling. Under the call of God they went to Israel and told them of their wickedness and need of repentance.

John the Baptist is exactly the same. He saw correctly and witnessed correctly and spoke correctly and lived correctly and died correctly. John 12:24 says that "The seed must die." Let us also see correctly: myself, the church, our present age.

Jerusalem is the clock of the world, and it indicates that these are the latter days. We are being called by a Macedonian call to many places asking for the Gospel before the time runs out. Every indication is that the clock stands at five minutes to twelve. All the prophecies in the Scripture are now fulfilled, except one— His return. We don't know how much longer we can proclaim the Gospel, so we must take advantage of every opportunity before it is too late.

It is far past time that we give the go signal to the training of national workers. Satanic power has never been so unleashed in world history as we find today. Already some Asian countries have closed the door to full-time missionaries from foreign countries. India, for example, with 500 million people, has plans to close its doors completely in the 1970's. According to authorities in government, by that time all foreign missionaries will be excluded from getting a visa.

Indonesia has shown a real revival through native workers. For this reason, many Bible institutes are now being started to train national workers, rather than sending foreigners to the front lines. I know many effective ministries that are changing their emphasis to national workers.

One aspect of this principle, of course, is to send aged to aged, beggar boy to beggar boy, blind to blind, orphan to orphan, prisoner to prisoner, because they understand their society and their type of person. Everyone with Jesus is a missionary and everyone without Him is a mission field. Our concern in missions is not areas only. Wherever we are, we are already missionaries for His kingdom. And the most obvious place to begin is with the kind of people we know best.

We have not heard such a cry of people for the Gospel since the world was created. This is your signal to go. Go with the Gospel.

§ "FROM MY HEART TO YOURS"

Do you remember my using the statement "We Christians never have problems just situations, according to Romans 8:28"? Well, I've had to practice what I've been preaching.

About two months ago Kathy became very ill. While she was lying in bed, unable to care for herself and family, I had two jobs: my preaching and dishwashing. The first job is familiar to me but the second one I hated. I'm almost certain that is why I became sick. I came down with pneumonia and had to cancel some of my meetings.

Kathy was given X rays which revealed that she had an ulcer. Not knowing a thing about cooking, it was not easy for me to prepare the foods necessary. Because she had never eaten these American foods before, it seemed right to me to give her what she wanted, Korean food. All of you who know what ulcers are, know that Korean food is the worst thing in the world for ulcers. It was during Kathy's illness that I came down with pneumonia. A blessing in disguise!

Oh, how I remembered what I'd been preaching all this time, "no problems just situations." Kathy and I are grateful to Mrs. Lea Powers, who is general secretary for our mission. She stepped into the situation and took over. She doubled as nurse and took care of us until we were on our feet again.

After being in bed for about forty-five days, Kathy went down to about ninety pounds. It was thought that she would have to go in the hospital. Because the costs of hospitals here are prohibitive, we decided that it might be better to send her to Korea for medical attention.

Praise the Lord for Dr. Charles Engel who has been taking care of both of us. Dr. Engel is a dedicated man of God and an outstanding doctor. He suggested that he should give Kathy more extensive tests before making a final decision concerning sending her to Korea. What a pleasant surprise when the X rays showed everything to be almost normal. Praise the Lord for doctors such as Dr. Engel, who are totally dedicated to Him and who seek His guidance concerning each and every patient. Under his wonderful care I improved rapidly also.

". . . Come ye yourselves apart into a desert place and rest a while; for there were many coming and going and they had no leisure so much as to eat" (Mark 6:31).

God wishes that we should set ourselves apart and rest awhile. When we do not know enough to do this for ourselves, sometimes it is done for us. Hallelujah! I was not only rested but the Lord dealt with me while I was laid aside with pneumonia. I found that more time must be spent in prayer and meditation, in order to be more effective for the Lord. What blessings I received. Do we really love Jesus? Do we walk with Him? I know that some of us are always doing, doing, doing.

It was during this time of refreshing that I received the answer on how to proceed with the Youth Ministry. This had been a burden on my heart since the beginning of the year.

Your "suitcase missionary" is back in full swing again in the high schools and churches. Kathy is getting along nicely. She is now able to care for her family again. Praise the Lord.

I wish to take this opportunity to thank all of you who have been praying for us. We thank you for all your cards and expressions of love. What a thrill to have Christian friends.

And this is an urgent call to prayer. I know that the Lord has opened doors for the school ministry, but we need your prayerful support. This is our opportunity to reach the youth with the Gospel in these last days.

Perhaps this special note from our All-Asia Association secretary shares the opportunity and burden of my heart:

"We are all familiar with the barriers set up in all of our schools to keep the Gospel out. Praise God that Ben has a foot in the door, as it were.

"Let me tell you one example: Just this past week, Ben spoke to 13,000 students in the Chaffey and Fontana Districts alone. What an opportunity we all have to help. Every time we pick up a newspaper and read of the conditions in our schools, we almost feel helpless. But we *know* that Christ can change lives.

"At each school meeting a card is passed out to each student. They then can request the message, in print, that Ben gave that day. Or they may request Ben's booklet, "No Longer an Orphan." This is our way of getting the name of the student. Then we follow up with literature telling the plan of salvation. All literature and Bible Correspondence Courses and pen-pal materials with Christian Koreans, were prepared while Ben was on a sick bed."

§ "FOUR THINGS GOD WANTS YOU TO BE"

There are hundreds of sermons and tracts telling us what God wants us to know and what God wants us to do. Without doubt they are important. But the Holy Spirit has often laid upon my heart to speak about the things God wants us to be. These are the precious aspects of His plan for the salvation of man.

First of all, *be honest with God*. Many men, at heart, find it difficult to be honest with each other and with themselves and with God. Even as we hide our vices from each other, we attempt to hide them from God.

With God's help, if we are strong enough to be completely honest, God will make it clear to us that we are in need of help. "For all have sinned" (Romans 3:23). That "all" includes everyone of us. By accepting this truth which comes directly from His Word, we come to realize that we need Christ.

When a husband or wife is not honest with the other partner, they are not capable of becoming a complete unit. The two remain two. So our relationship with God is incomplete unless we are submissive and honest enough to admit to Him, and ourselves, what we really are as persons. Honesty with God is the very basis of salvation. It acts as a cleansing instrument, cutting away the foreign matter accumulated around the heart, and exposes a renewed and cleansed soul.

One is often indignant when the issue of personal salvation is put before him. "I'm all right," he rationalizes. "I am good to my family, I work hard, and I've never committed a major crime." Then why is our world in such a deplorable state if its people are all right? Honesty with God will bring about an enlightenment. We will be shown that we "come short of the glory of God," and then will come to recognize our need of Him and His way of pardoning our pasts and guaranteeing our futures.

Secondly, *be born again* by the water and the Spirit. "Water" in Biblical phraseology refers to the Word of God. Through the Word of God we must repent, must recognize our ungodly habits and ways and turn around to Him.

Just as a fish must be born in the water to live in the water, and a man must be born on the earth to live on the earth, so our soul must be "born in the spirit" to live in a spiritual world now, and ultimately in heaven. Through repentance we are blessed with a "second birth." This spiritual birth produces our spiritual life.

Thirdly, *be filled with the Holy Spirit.* After we have become "believers" we have the problem of self to obliterate. It is the self that interferes with our being truly submissive to God. Our old habits and attitudes which are incongruous with the Christian way of life have to be sublimated and controlled. It will take real humbling of our selves to come to this place of decision. Of course, the Bible promises that the humble shall be honored: "Whosoever therefore shall humble himself as this little child, the same is the greatest in the kingdom of heaven" (Matthew 18:4). We must be saved from self through the power of the risen Saviour! In other words: Self must be crucified.

The Lord asks our willing obedience: "I beseech you therefore, brethren, by the mercies of God, that ye present your bodies a living sacrifice, holy, acceptable unto God, which is your reasonable service" (Romans 12:1). But even though He requests it, He does not leave us helpless in attaining righteousness through our natural efforts. He gives us a soul mate, the Holy Spirit. "When he, the Spirit of truth, is come, he will guide you into all truth" (John 16:13). The gift of the Holy Spirit is given when we are "born again." Through the work of the Holy Spirit in our lives, we will come to a full knowledge of being God's child.

Let us cite a few truths about the function of the Holy Spirit. The Holy Spirit is the third part of the Trinity which God places in the heart of those who come to a knowledge of the saving grace of Jesus Christ our Lord. The possession of the Holy Spirit in one's life is His gift to us as our companion as we walk in the way of the Lord.

But there must be a constant rededication of our lives to the Lord. There must be a daily prayer request that we be "filled" with the Holy Spirit continually. We, through our faith, must ask to be refilled, knowing that He will accomplish it as a result of our faith and submission to Him. This request for "refilling" has to be made on a day to day, hour by hour, even moment by moment supplication through our prayers.

This "filling" energizes and sustains us as we let Him work out His will through our lives. "Be filled with the Spirit," cried the Apostle Paul (Ephesians 5:18). "Filling" is not to be a once-in-a-lifetime experience, but rather it is a continual source of power for the believer. It acts as our buffer to outside forces which seek to break us down. We must ask for filling through faith and it is conditional upon our submission to God.

Live for Christ today by appropriating His gifts each day. Yesterday's calendar is lost for eternity, but today is a clean white page to be used to its ultimate. Call upon the Holy Spirit to direct you daily, hourly, whereby you may experience the blessings the Lord has for you each day. Now, what we are now, today, this minute, is important to God—not our vague promises of how we'll perform tomorrow. Reading His Word daily, and calling upon the Holy Spirit to direct our paths, means "now." Now is our great responsibility.

Fourth, *be yielded to the Lord.* Trust Him totally. "Totally" is not ninety-nine percent. One hundred percent surrender to God is the secret of a victorious Christian life. Faith, complete trust, no thought of doubt, will prove that Jesus never fails any one of us. Total submission to His will is a thrilling experience as we watch Him work through our lives. Yielded hearts mirror His omniscience, His omnipresence, and His omnipotence. The promises of His Word come into total fruition as our knowledge of Him travels from the intellect to the heart.

James instructs us that our yielding to the Lord will help us in overcoming the influences of the world and satanic forces: "Submit yourselves therefore to God. Resist the devil, and he will flee from you" (James 4:7). What a great promise a yielded soul may claim. Not submission merely, but total submission, a squelching of the old self and its appetites, moment by moment, will produce miracle upon miracle in your life. Peace will be yours. Eternal life is the ultimate great reward He offers for your obedience. Is there a greater reward in the universe? He is challenging you to enjoy His promise.

In closing, forgive me for a personal illustration from my family life. I have two boys: John is six, a quiet and good boy; Paul is four, and is a live wire who makes trouble (like me). One day we three were at the swimming pool. I was in the water and the two boys were standing on the edge.

I wanted them to practice swimming with their dad, so I said to them: "Would you like to jump to me here in the water?" They both agreed. Because the oldest is always first in Korea, I told John he might have the first opportunity.

John said: "Daddy, you mean me first?"

"Yes," I replied, "you first."

"Daddy, are you ready?"

I noticed he wanted to jump to me seventy-five percent, but he was hanging on the rail twenty-five percent. So I said, "Yes, I'm ready. Jump."

He responded: "Daddy, you're a little too far away."

My purpose was the practice, so I told John to wait and let Paul have his chance.

The minute I nodded to him, Paul said, "Daddy, me" and he just jumped. I grabbed him because I love him. No father would let his son fall down into the swimming pool.

Now I said again to John, "John, it's your turn."

Still he hesitated: "Daddy, do you love me?"

"Yes, I do."

He said with a smile: "Come closer."

I came closer two steps. He wanted to make sure, so he asked once again: "Are you ready?"

Now he wished to jump ninety-five percent and hang to the guard rail only five percent. I was a little disgusted, so I insisted he jump. I saw tears coming up in his eyes. I knew his heart. He wanted to jump ninety-nine percent, but he never did.

I don't like to see this wishing to jump, but still hanging on the rail one percent. Almost jumping is not good enough. This reminds me of the rich man who came to Jesus and asked how he could be saved. He almost became a disciple, but worldly things held him back enough so he didn't leave all and follow Jesus. An "almost marriage" is not too good! I would hate to have my wife love me seventy-five percent and another fellow twenty-five percent.

God loves you one hundred percent and needs your love in return one hundred percent. Yes, you are nice Christians and good church members. You serve the Lord in many ways. You don't make trouble in society and church. But how about total commitment to God? Are you a Christian who is still hanging on the rail twenty-five percent, ten percent, or even one percent?

Why don't you jump, by faith? Throw yourself into His mighty hands. Let go and let God! How happy you will be if you jump into God's hand. Total commitment is the secret of a victorious Christian life. If you jump to God by faith, He never fails you. Do it now!

VICTOR VALLEY JOINT UNION HIGH SCHOOL DISTRICT

VICTOR VALLEY
SENIOR HIGH SCHOOL

P. O. BOX 910

VICTORVILLE, CALIFORNIA 92392

Telephone (714) 245-9374

KEITH GUNN, Principal

May 2, 1968

To Whom It May Concern:

Just by chance, Mr. Ben Song came to my office on April 30, and offered his services as a speaker before our students. He wanted to do this in appreciation for having received his education through a gift of $10.00 per month made to him, a Korean orphan, by an American donor.

I have been associated with young men and women in the public schools for almost forty years and I can say without hesitation that I have never seen another person captivate his audience as Mr. Song has done today. He talked in three separate assemblies in our gymnasium, to the sophomores, juniors and the seniors. The seniors gave Mr. Song a standing ovation at the close of his talk which is the first time in the history of our school that this has taken place.

To anyone who wishes an inspired, down-to-earth speaker, I would unhesitatingly recommend Mr. Song. Our senior class has invited him back to speak to them in their government classes, such is their admiration for his ability as a speaker.

Keith Gunn, Principal

KG:b

February 2, 1968

To Whom It May Concern:

It is a pleasure to introduce to you this visitor from South Korea
who has appeared before many high school and college departments and
assemblies in California and Arizona. Reports from these addresses
would indicate that he is a most fascinating speaker whose personal
history and informative ideas create exceptional interest among our
youth.

Mr. Song is a high-type christian gentleman who feels impelled to
express the gratitude of his people to the citizens of the United
States. As more nations join the "hate America" group, it is
refreshing to learn of the lasting friendship of the people of
South Korea.

Sincerely yours,

Herschel Hooper, Director
Secondary Education

HH:gal